Rabbi Schlotz Talks With God

Michael Thomas

Rabbi Schlotz Talks With God

By,
Michael Thomas

Shoestring Book Publishing,
Maine USA

Rabbi Schlotz
Talks With God

Published by; Shoestring Book Publishing.

Copyright 2018
By, Michael Thomas

Paperback

ISBN: 978-1-943974-72-6
Library of Congress Control Number: 2018936741

Cover: God the Father - (Giovan Francesco Barbieri) (1591 - 1666)
Printed in the
United States of America.

Layout and design by Shoestring Book Publishing

For information address;
shoestringpublishing4u@gmail.com
www.shoesrtringbookpublishing.com

Acknowledgements:

This book is dedicated to my publishers, Allan Emery and Alison Emery of Shoestring Book Publishing, who exceed the boundaries of protocol by being my mentors, advisors, friends and ultimately the best publishers I could have ever expected to find.

To trust someone who understands words and their power, is to lay the sword down and accept that which is greater by far. My thanks to both of you, Allan and Alison.

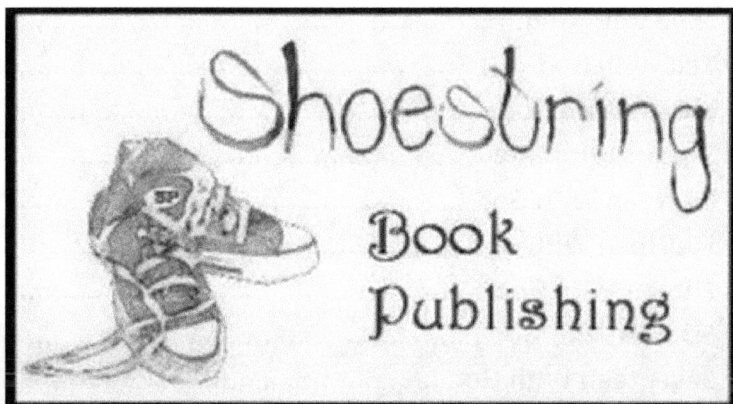

Table of Contents

Editorial Preface:

Don't let the title fool you. This is not really a religious book. You will not be lead to salvation, probably. This is more of a study in possibilities. If you could talk to God, what would you say? How would he respond? My personal belief is that the conversation would be individualistic for each and every person.

So, here is one of them. I have taken the liberty of putting the words of God in Bold. This way, the reader will have no trouble knowing who said what.

The author uses the interjection: *Interlude* from time to time to denote that time has passed and that he has been thinking. Naturally, God is always up to speed on what he is thinking. So it is OK to go straight into an unrelated conversation after an interlude.

Editor

Day One With God

Rabbi:
I had this encounter with god. I mean, like, we were in a poetry class and the teacher was a bald, middle age, married man who made a whistling sound when he talked, like he was running out of air in his lungs.

God sat slouched. He seemed bemused by his pencil having an eraser. I threw him a look and he, sort of, smiled or winced - I was not sure what it was he did with his face, but it was not mean.

I whispered to him: "Are you taking this class for credit?" He hesitated:

God:
"Just to see what they are saying about poetry. I already know the answers, but I am curious."

Rabbi:
"Is that something about you, that you are curious? Curious about this and other things?"

He smiled this time, and nodded without giving me an answer.

Now God is not an imposing figure. He has brown hair and the look as if his heritage embodied a mix marriage. He defied singularity but posed an enigmatic dichotomy of skin texture similar to a shorn sheep's hide. All during the time, he kept turning his pencil in his hand, letting the eraser end tap gently on the desk top.

Rabbi:
"Is there a reason for so much pain on the earth? It seems that is all that is in the news - bad news."

God:
"I do not know what to tell you. People have free will."

Rabbi: "Is that what you are putting in your poem?"

God:
"What do you want me to say? Free will; it's obvious."

Rabbi:
"What is the corollary? Opposite of free will?"

God:
"Free will is like a cat that decides to run away from home and then either gets comfortable in the wild, or regrets having run away."

Rabbi:
"How blasé."

God:
"Blasé?"

Rabbi:
"Indifferent."

God:
(Puzzled) "Indifferent?"

Rabbi:
"Tell me, what about the people who consider themselves victims? Where is their free will?"

God:
"They never lost it. It's still there."

Rabbi:
"What if they are born crippled?"

God:
"They still have free will to choose their kind of lifestyle."

Rabbi:
"Choose? How do you choose a life? Ha, choose!"

God:
"You obviously do not understand reincarnation. I cannot bring you up to speed on everything in this one poetry class."

Day Two With God

Rabbi:
Why did you create so many wonderful written works that we can never get around to reading if we had six hundred lifetimes?

God:
I had them created and reading them is your problem.

Rabbi:
But, what good are they, like the "Vedas" or Mallory's "Le Morte Darthur" or James George Frazer's "The Golden Bough"?

God:
They are good.

Rabbi:
Good! But too much. I think you do these things to test our patience.

God:
I do not do them. I have no reason to test you. You are your own test. I will tell you this. I can read and absorb in a flash. I do enjoy what you have created with the talents I have given you.

Interlude

Rabbi
Hey, wake up. What's the deal. They are playing Bach
Cantata BWV29

God:
I have heard it.

Rabbi
Well, hearing it again won't hurt you. It is so beautiful.

God:
Got it. I agree it is very lovely.

Rabbi
Gedenk an uns mit deiner Leibe

God:
You humans, get so sour faced when the music is in the
German.

Rabbi
It was Bach's language.

God:
Language of the intellectuals of the time.

Rabbi
What do you prefer in heaven?

God:
Plain talk. Like the street language of New York or Tokyo. My favorite language is how they speak in the series "The Wire". I like how the black thugs twist words and images poetically. It is an indication of how language evolves by common usage.

Interlude

The Rigveda Hymn 1:35. Savitar (modeled)
Agni ....I call upon Mitra, Varuna, to aid us here..........
Come cool breeze morning laying itself lazy upon shadow's darkness escaping wherewithal willy-nilly beneath leaf sleep covered bramble thickets.

Collect thyself bundled bright hurled into horizons of welcome voices.

Let heaven be recreated over turbulent ocean waves quelled by thy voice, oh Asura, kind leader of goodness excelled by no one.

Watch little eyes peek from distant foliage in wonder at your brightness aglow with strength beyond the mists of time.

Upon the earth's eight points converging in a path of woven brilliance like sparkling skeins of yarn burning with no fire but only electric atoms - Let this be your bequest to points of our enlightenment.

Day Three With God

Rabbi:
What are you listening to?

God:
Brahms.

Rabbi:
Doesn't he get redundant?

God:
Nothing gets tedious unless you filter your expectations. Pay attention clearly.

Rabbi:
He was a tormented soul.

God:
All my creations have torments.

Rabbi:
Does it make you feel superior if we are inferior?

God:
I expect you to return to me some measure of creation regardless of what wolves howl at your door. Brahms did the best he could but he always felt inferior to Beethoven. All composers after Beethoven fell short of him.

Rabbi:
Why did you make Beethoven so powerful?

God:
I did not make him do anything. He broke out of the mundane with his own will and revolutionized music.

Rabbi:
If you liked Beethoven so much, why did you make him deaf

God:
He chose deafness as an impetus to excel.

Rabbi
Where is he now, after he died?

God:
In a quiet garden listening to the sounds of nature fill his heart with the happiness of having his hearing back. You have a lot of questions for one who has many roads yet to travel. I am reminded of Vincent van Gogh chiding a painter to paint and quit looking at him with amazement. My Vincent knew the temporariness of reality and how delicate the moment was to paint from his deep inner places.

interlude

Before moments pass into hours, days into time's canyons, let thy heart open as wide as mouths can to swallow eternity.

Thy feet shall not outrun the sun. Nor shall thy soul outpace my lessons. Speed into life with desperation for thy shall best face death with a hammer in thy hand or a mind engraved with all beauty.

Day Four With God

Interlude

I danced in the morning when the world had begun
I danced in the moon and the stars and the sun
I came down from heaven and I danced on the earth
At Bethlehem I had my birth.

Dance, dance, wherever you may be
I am the lord of the dance, said he
And I lead you all, wherever you may be
And I lead you all in the dance, said he
'Tis the gift to be simple,
'Tis the gift to be free.

'Tis the gift to come down
Where we ought to be.
And when we find ourselves
In the place just right,
'Twill be in the valley
Of love and delight.

Dance, dance, wherever you may be
I am the lord of the dance, said he
And I lead you all, wherever you may be
And I lead you all in the dance, said he.

When true simplicity is gained,
To bow and to bend

We shall not be ashamed.
To turn, turn
Will be our delight,
'Till by turning, turning
We come round right.

Dance, dance, wherever you may be
I am the lord of the dance, said he
And I lead you all, wherever you may be
And I lead you all in the dance, said he.

I danced in the morning when the world had begun
I danced in the moon and the stars and the sun
I came down from heaven and I danced on the earth
At Bethlehem I had my birth.

Dance, dance, wherever you may be
I am the lord of the dance, said he
And I lead you all, wherever you may be
And I lead you all in the dance, said he.

Dance, dance, wherever you may be
I am the lord of the dance, said he
And I lead you all, wherever you may be
And I lead you all in the dance, said he.

Interlude

Rabbi:
You are God singing such an old song.

God:
Yes.

Rabbi:
Why?

God:
Out of such simple things I build mountains.

Rabbi:
I would be thinking that you would be entertained by choruses.

God:
Goes to show you.

Rabbi:
I have a question - What is the reason for all the myths of Greek and Roman gods who interact with human natures embodied with deific natures?

God:
Those can be considered the early attempts to define me. I, of course, have nothing to do with the development of religions. They are there and I enjoy understanding them.

Rabbi:
Do you have a family?

God:
I am God and will leave that to you to figure out.

Interlude

Here where my family sacrificed to settle birthplace
as time waited slow sun rising over heavens space;

Here glorious voices rang out collecting silences strung.
Oh! My father who enriched earth with seed; Mother
giving tearful screams as I emerged between her legs
like a helpless bird with no knowledge but her teat.

Let all creation slide away from me as I sleep
enduring growth of flowers attached to my dreams.

Day Five With God

Rabbi:
My right hip hurts / if I die who will care?

God:
You are so boring.

Rabbi:
And so are you.

God:
"If you die!" Do you realize how insignificant you are? There are billions of souls scrunched together on this small earth. There is no stopping them from choosing such an easy location to manifest their ineptitude.

Rabbi:
Well, what are you doing here?

God:
I happen to like Charles Ives. His Trio for violin, cello and piano is marvelous.

Rabbi:
I simply cannot believe you. You are here listening to a minor composer ...

God:
Stop it!. You wake up and indulge yourself in self-pity about dying and I will not let you denigrate Charles Ives. He made so much use of the abilities I endowed him with. It is beyond your understanding to appreciate the mixture of joy and sadness that makes up his music. Sometimes I want to just get rid of earth and all you lazy thinking souls scratching your lives away like chickens. By the way, bonehead, your right hip is beginning to become weak. You are close to eighty years old and you do not have much more time left with the body you have. You should be thankful that you have had so many good years with very little pain. Go back to sleep.

Interlude

3 Moderato Con Moto / Trio for violin, cello & piano /
Charles Ives

Reshape thyself in velvet green under-wood
Left decayed between twig, leaf, mixture of sad moistness

Motion trilled wrenched asunder intrepid piano
Spacing itself around violin and cello

Cool as color never changing to dew dampness
How innocently aged music
Gift of strength savagely entangled
Bemused in lace and lintel aperture
Bold yet submissive sound of elegance

Reshape thyself in vegetation

This is what is left over from love
Like fallen limbs denuded of leaf
Escaping in solitude of imposed biers
Listen - tears of pools / angst of regret
Little did you know sorrow until now.

Day Six With God

Interlude

Veda Hymn 10:81 Visvakarman

He who sat down as Hotar-priest, the Rishi, our father, offering up all things existing.

Kala powers the cosmic wheel of time (kala-cakra) upon which the effulgent chariot of Surya (the sun-god-) moves thorough the heavens, illuminating the universe and making the passage of hours, days and years.

The pole star is the center of the zodiacal wheel and remains fixed while the equator moves quickly: Sagittarius, Capricorn, Aquarius, Pisces, Aries, Taurus, Gemini, Cancer, Leo, Virgo, Libra, Scorpio. In Hindu tradition, the twelve houses are known as "Bhavas:"

Whence Visvakarman, seeing all, producing the earth, with mighty power hath eyes on all sides round about him, a mouth on all sides, arms and feet on all sides, he, the sole god producing earth and heaven, weldeth them, with his arms as wings, together.

God:
Beautiful.

Rabbi:
Agreed.

Interlude

Whence come I from between the legs of my mother in cries
resounding up to the heavens in sorrow for my birth upon a
bitter hungry earth waiting, immediately, to devour me
in so few years.

Sleep, sleep so soundlessly upon thy manger of straw.
Tomorrow as Helios awakens dawn ceaselessly bringing
us morning.

Then about thyself I shall gird you with garments of silk in aromatic perfumes sufficing all desires in exultation and harmony.

Father of my seed instilled within me a basic strength to allow me grow as you wish for your furtherance through me. I shall always sing praise for you upon imaginary altars of grace.

God:
Where are you taking this?

Rabbi:
Not sure.

God:
Get on with it.

Interlude

Rabbi:
So many beliefs. Each extolling gods of creation. For myself, I watch the passing of moons upon the darkened tree tops and pray as thanks for such instruments of solace within my soul.

God:
As you should, always.

Rabbi:
Remember that thou art always god and I can change whenever I wish. You, God, are the center of the wheel of time and I am

the round-a-bout servant of your wishes. I bow to your
supremacy and bend my knee to you.

Day Seven With God

Rabbi:
Sometimes small things become huge upon reflection. Someone told me: :"Choose your battles wisely:" So many times I have been faced with impropriety. When anger wells up, I stop and decide what is the best path - Do I pursue or let things work themselves out without my intervention. I am not sure, but when I leave things to the fates, they usually get resolved in my favor. I have no doubt that some form of resolution is taking place in an undercurrent of divine manner.

God:
You have a lot to say today. And, you are correct - If you wait, you shall be rewarded. Buddha taught patience. Have you forgotten?

Rabbi:
Time is a very subtle agent of change. I heard said: The only thing constant on the face of the earth is change. If everything is in flux why do we even trust the present?

God:
O ye of little faith.

Rabbi:
Was that quote from Luke 12:28?

God:
You know your New Testament.

Rabbi:
The thing you forget is that humanity has a short fuse when a quick solution is a strong urge.

"It is mine to avenge; I will repay:" says the Lord.

Interlude

Summer thunder passes quickly over-land. Rain dries, clouds part, sun sweeps back from hiding - bright, now, over the dew.

Today's sorrows disappear as tomorrow erases all our fears.
I am beholden to the Lord for wheels of joy bringing deliverance.

Day Eight With God

Veda Hymn 7:30. Indra

With power and strength, O Mighty God, approach us: be the augmenter, Indra, of these riches; Strong Thunderer, Lord of men, for potent velour, for manly exploit and for high dominion. Thee, worth invoking, in the din of battle, heroes invoke in fray for life and sunlight. Among all people thou art foremost fighter: give up our enemies to easy slaughter ...

(Recast)

With softness in our hearts we call upon thee like quiet fern waving listless in wind through forest vales. Peace collects inside our souls in parcels of solitude. We make of the world a background to our prayers.

Give us, O Indra, over to whisper of willow trees leaning as strands of silver reflection of branches loosing themselves to a mysterious song without words.

Lift from our shoulders burdens of life. Ease those weights of sorrows to make them as cottonwood fluff wafting through currents of motion aimlessly.

Day Nine With God

Interlude

Veda Adhuyaya 31.

Purusha hath a thousand heads, a thousand eyes, a thousand feet. Pervading earth on every side he fills a space ten fingers broad.
When he rose up three fourths remained and three fourths went forward on both sides of earth and heaven.

Purusha whose color is like the sun, beyond the reach of darkness. He only who knows him leaves death behind...................There is no path save this alone to travel.

Recast

Before the sides of heaven, stretch I discomfited. Never will I fill the vessel of light or cavity of darkness as you, my god, can do.

I think and my thoughts evaporate into dust of deserts. When I become enamored with myself thy presence erupts to swallow my soul to naught.

Thy colors vibrate into choral antipodes above and below the spiral of suns girth. Halo circles stars in their path of silence. How emanations of universal murmurs fills me with peace.

Let thy doors open to expanses beyond my sight. Come to me as if winds tracked my heart. Beside mansions of turrets with banners swaying gaily, I bow in reverence to thy presence.

Day Ten With God

Rabbi:

It is time to worry. We have a cute gay cherub in charge of North Korea. We have a misfired fire-cracker posing president never in the White House. We have a dis-jointed, fractured group of congressional geese eating microphones on white house grass waiting for hurricane season to start or pass.

We, who think, think in dismay over an untenable set of circumstances in America or world stage, like a ship of dunces doing their best to unhinge all of us with boy scout behavior.

Surely Spock can save the enterprise, maybe. But one thing is for sure neither Noam Chomsky nor (dead) B F Skinner can put Humpty Dumpty back together again.

Raise the Arizona: Sell raw steel to Japan; Bury the voice of T S Eliot reciting Wasteland on a New York street corner where three million people are waiting for a change of light so they can look before they cross.

Forgive us, please, for our sins of ego run rampant over reason. Bring back Washington Irving's Sleepy Hollow for the headless horseman's riding with a lantern and shouting that the British are coming by the sea. "By the sea. By the sea. By the beautiful sea. You and me, you and me, o how happy we'll be"

God:
Oh! Boy!

Day Eleven With God

Rabbi:
Soft brilliance speckled
Your face remains clear
In memory bedazzled
Blue eyed madam dear

Yesterday's bright hue
A canvas in relief
Turns all that I knew
To joy away from grief

Madam dear alight
Cloudless mystery
Aligned in a tight
Timeless history

God:
Poet's insufficiency Love can override
A god 's jealousy No place to hide
Little is left to see Angels close eyes
Glow of deity Humanity's surprise
We can only wait Watch patiently
A time constraint Betrays eternity

Day Twelve With God

Rabbi:
I am sick and tired of life
I wake up a half person
Age overcomes me
Go to hell with this life

God:
It takes bravery.

Rabbi:
Screw your indifference
What the hell to you have to worry about
You are the great, great God who lives forever

God:
You have no idea what I have to go through to be God.

Rabbi:
You have no idea how disgusting life is when health fails
I cannot stand all the peace and beauty that surrounds me.
What good does it do to live morally righteous?
What good is all the effort I put into being kind to people around me?

God:
Pity poor me.

Rabbi:

On top of all this death and decay, we still do not know what happens to us when we die. Your life plan sucks.

God:

Some of my greatest subjects faced life with excellent analysis.

Interlude

O life with all your beauty, fall behind me
forward facing bits of comfort squeezed between compacted
clay, dried decay
none of your homilies or preaching can overcome my disgust
smells of wasting away draw out worms and maggots
all great edifices crumble into dust
a wind of fierceness blows creation into a crevice of silence
voices of languish and fervor recede to murmurs
too distant to hear
all of history tumbles into wasted horizons where remembrance
exists only as a whoosh of non-existence
here is where nothing resides in unformed emptiness
we humans follow soundless corridors of bleakness
we divest ourselves of thought
we become armies of ghosts who leave a world of calamities to
enter a world of barren blindness - a world of formlessness and
forlorn quintessential vacuumed zilch
a world of dreamless wandering void of hope
who will remember dawns of days merged into night
great interludes of creation where emerging whales are born in
floating nurseries of fish and fauna

stillness of a doe resting beside its mother in afterbirth on forest
brambles of broken twigs and crumbling leaf beds
why were we given a Renaissance
why needing orchestrated music to see it go to waste
left over menus tasteless and blank
wondrous words of philosophers melting upon evaporating
pages where libraries tumble to sifted sands

Day Thirteen With God

God:
You finally turned the television off.

Rabbi:
Yes.

God:
I have been waiting.

Rabbi:
What are you listening to?

God:
Janine Jansen's album of Schubert String Quintet in C major, D956.

Rabbi:
Is she the only performer?

God:
Also: Boris Brovtsyn violinist, Amhai Grosz, Jens Peter Maintz, Maxim Rysanov violists and Torleif Thedeen on cello.

Rabbi:
You are God and how do you keep up with these modern performers and their new albums?

God:
It is your job to keep up with me.

Rabbi:
Schubert is highly emotional. His music always has that tinge of sorrow in each piece he composes. Some call Schubert sentimental.

God:
The reason I like Schubert is his increasingly meditative "dark side of the human psyche with a deeper sense of spiritual awareness" and his conception of the "beyond".

Rabbi:
Isn't spiritual awareness the goal of most all classical music composers?

God:
Yes, you have a point.

Rabbi:
What is your favorite piece of classical music?

God:
I like all music. I have no favorite. My favorite piece of music is the one I happen to be listening to in the immediate moment.

Interlude

When snow blends into shadows among rocks sloped across
ridges spreading by degrees of distances rising up to mountains
disappearing shaded into grey cloud horizons, there is my heart
bled white.
There in the muted sunless crevices I sit and hear cellos calling
out wishes of somber strings. Let dancers sleep. Let low bands
of angels rest till dawn. I am mixed in with flowerless
sentiments. I am strung like prayer beads circling heaven's
environs.

Day Fourteen With God

Rabbi:
Consider earth 4.5 billion years old.

Consider homo sapiens (us) becoming the most dominant species 6, 000 years ago.

Consider five mass extinctions in earth's 4.5 billion years, all caused by natural catastrophes.

Consider that we live as arrogant egotistical species, who have created the conditions for the absolute sixth mass extinction to arrive very soon.

All our talk, books, music, civilizations, endeavors will fold into dust and be gone for good in a very immediate future.

How lucky we are to be able to look into the future as well as look into the present and past all within our grasp.

We write, talk, conjecture about things, yet we are on the path to extinction no matter how we twist facts or reinterpret circumstances.

Our religions, recently formulated are compendiums of all religions from past till now. All rituals and customs have been inherited from all past beliefs. The Jesus we have was the Sun God they had. The Mohammad they have is the Jesus others had. The Buddha they had came from the Confucius that China had. The Confucius China had came from the Gilgamesh out of the tales of histories. You can look upon religions on a straight line with all beliefs remaining the same throughout history. The basic belief all strung through time is:

> Love your neighbor as you self and love and respect the mysterious beings who created all nature around us.

Our heritage will be remembered in its futility to not be able to sustain our hopes and dreams.

I have published over thirteen books. More are coming. Yet, I am stupid; More stupid than a stone. More stupid than a forest fire or a sun that cannot speak itself other than its show-and-tell procession every morning and every night in sanguine despondency.

Day Fifteen With God

The Rabbi is feeling emotional tonight.

In 1965 the Rabbi refused to go to the field ceremony to get awarded a purple heart.

At age nineteen, he knew there was no honor in medals. He also knew his injury was small. Among all the things the Rabbi knew, the most foremost was that he could never be part of any group. He even distanced himself from patriotism.

Here is how he viewed Vietnam: The Americans were fool enough to not learn a thing from the French being driven out of Vietnam.

The Rabbi was assigned to Vietnam at his request because the Army would not send him anywhere but a one year assignment which corresponded to his one year remaining on his enlistment of three years.

In Vietnam the Rabbi was finance sergeant of the 52nd Aviation Battalion. He slept in foxholes at night and did office work all day.

Once released, he went straight home to Detroit and remained linked to the city of his birth all his life.

Rabbi came home to obscurity. All his uncles and family had come home from World War II with honors and recognition. Rabbi came home to a Coney Island hot dog and solitude.

God:
What did you expect?

Rabbi:
Nothing! I am just glad to be alive and working.

God:
Good.

Day Sixteen With God

Interlude

We die in scoops of life
rising to surface cooling
in pots of existence.

We die with our raspy tears
regrets for deeds unchanging
but for solace and sorrows.

Little rosaries of time lapses,
small capsules of sacred sins:
We die, die unforgiven.
World's too busy to intercede.

Sun brings joy of mornings without our reverie.
Night mists cover over where we once stood.
Airs nocturnal receding savors of aromas,
leave a space for strange creatures to breathe.

Tomorrow a guitar will strum minor chords of bleakness.
Let the talisman foretell disaster of exhumed fumes.
Let fortune tellers be lost for words.
Tea leaves blurred.
No expectations.
Horizons evaporated.
Exclusive societies of worms.

Rabbi:
Why all this history of upheaval and pain?
Bibles of disbelief in torture, destruction
how can we trust in a God that allows such?

God:
Your histories are yours, not mine.

Rabbi:
You have no guilt?

God:
Absolutely none what-so-ever. Two roads were placed before your ancestors. Same two roads you are faced with. Let's not talk about which path you will take. I watch. I am patience exemplified.

interlude

You die in groups.
All alone friendless.
By yourself facing
Headless horsemen with swords, balls and chains.

Somewhere in lands without borders.
Distances short yet eternities stretched.
Sweetness turned sour.
Hope pushed out by

Black projections.

Interlude

Father and mother
laid where others lay
Here in daydreams
I pray to you today

Father and mother
left me to unwind
all pain and sorrow
days dark unkind

Gods and angels
watching, waiting
for souls wandering
grace so everlasting

Mother and father
cheer us in hope
days strangled
fate's bound rope

Father and mother
bye and bye tears
dry up our eyes
take all our fears

Give us fake Jesus
disciples and prophets
saints stranded alone
we are spirit puppets.

Father and mother
we decry your words
here without you
silences are heard

Day Seventeen With God

Rabbi:
I have managed to remain free of moneyed people who have crossed my life.

God:
Is this a bragging session?

Rabbi:
Listen, at least I am not an alcoholic, drug addict, miser...........

God:
Bla bla bla. The list goes on and on.......

Rabbi:
Seriously. Some very famous and rich people have tried to induce me into their private worlds.

God:
So, what do you want from me right now? You want me to recognize....

Rabbi:
Yeah! Placate me a little. Tell me you know my situation. You are God and know everything.

God:

Humans are such fools, you included. When you can forgive and move on to greater levels of spiritualism, then you will be serving your karma.

Rabbi:

Who the hell do I need to forgive? My ex-wife? She is an idiot full of delusional self-pity. She thinks herself a victim.

God:

Forgive her for being human.

Rabbi:

How in the hell do you forgive a woman who for fifty years still carries hatred toward me. I have tried my best to treat her kindly and she cannot even talk to me. She is exactly the same person who she was fifty years ago.

God:

Let her go in your mind. Let her go silly man. You are exactly the same person you were fifty years ago. Let yourself go. Let the past be buried in the tunnel of your memory.

Look. You are an intelligent well centered person. You follow leads and learn new viewpoints every day. Why do you even want your ex-wife as a friend? You do not have any other friends? Just include her in the schematic of your isolationism. Problem is that you are bogged down by wanting her to change. You have no right to want her to be different than she is. You need to keep on being different and forget her.

You know, you seem to have forgotten that you have two very wonderful balanced children that came out of your, so called, "bad marriage".

It was not a bad marriage. It was good. Tell me, what would you have done with your time fifty years ago when you needed to get over the idea of marriage and go on with your life? You did exactly what was necessary. Tell me, again, if you shop at a new supermarket, do you get angry at the one you abandoned?

Rabbi:
You are silly.

Day Eighteen With God

Rabbi:
My family was indistinct.
They all withered like fall flowers.
Like last winter snow spilling itself into dirty spring
City Street drains.

All the juice of becoming an adult came to me and never did
they recognize neither their poetics nor mine.

First, my father was benign. A large man over three hundred
pounds. He carried his weight well. He was a big man all his life.
Not gross fat, just heavy. Typically, like a Buddha waiting for
wisdom to fill him in. It never came. Yet he was cordial to
people. Generous. Proud of his prominence that he imagined,
but could not define. He stood out when I saw him among his
peers. Uncle Johnny was braggadocio, my dad was understated
and quiet, almost half asleep. Uncle Joe was always making
statements about my dad to which my dad would look Joe in the
eye and say, "Is that right?" It was funny the way my dad would
look at Joe then turn his eyes back down to his cards to analyze
his hand, simply ignoring Joe with indifference.

Uncle Rocco would set his cards face down and swear at Johnny
and Joe to leave my "Partner alone". Rocco would point to the
card my dad laid down and remind Johnny and Joe that whether
my dad was asleep or awake, he had played the right card.

My father seemed to have the idea that he deserved to be waited on. My mother would cater to him. I do not think that he was lazy, just self-deserving. My father was like a potentate or czar. I used to imagine him as Falstaff from Henry VII by Shakespeare. But a Falstaff with no chicanery or cleverness.

Funny thing about him was that he never said anything wise. But, he never said anything much at all, he just watched carefully then would fall asleep ignoring the people around him.

It took years of me growing up to appreciate my father's ineffectual ways. I think that my love for him became full bloom when I begin to see him clearer or see him in the round like a statute.

Why are you so quiet?

God:
I am listening. I am glad you learned to love your father.

Rabbi:
Did you go through a learning curve with your father?

Day Nineteen With God

Rabbi:
Thank you for being here with me.

God:
I am always with you.

Rabbi:
Please, do not get overly dramatic with me.

God:
Amen, Amen I say to you ...

Rabbi:
Shut up! I have things I need to talk about.

God:
Talk.

Rabbi:
You know, I am a pretty good writer. But, I do not write too much fiction.

God:
Why do you think that?

Rabbi:
Why I do not write fiction?

God:
Yeah, ok.

Rabbi:
It was, kind of, a question to you. But, I think I know the answer: Fiction writers make believe and they throw in important dogma or discussion as a side issue to their fictional characters and plots.

I write from the points of view of real situations, mostly.

But, you know, there is an element of my writing and that is: That I write a lot about my family.

I guess, my family is important to me because I spend a lot of time analyzing how I compare to them or understand them, primarily.

God:
Is this all you wanted to talk about tonight?

Rabbi:
My mother was very important to me at different times in her life. As her first born child, she lavished a lot of attention on me during my childhood years. She turned me into her little servant who knew how to polish, clean and organize her house. And, in those early years of her marriage, she had not lost her youthful vigor, although she was on the road to give up swimming and all the excitement of her hopes and dreams. She and I listened to all the post war romantic songs on the radio, and we would sing together to our favorites. After time, she had three more

children who took up most of her time feeding, dressing and enduring. Those children never had the same relationship with her that I had.

But, of course, that all came to an end as I got older and began to develop areas away from her. When she realized that I stepped past that early imprinting, she began to resist my wanting independence. In fact, the more she resisted, the more I rebelled.

You know, God, which is typical that the stringency plays against the loosening of bonds. The more she tried to hold me, the more I got further and further away from her demands.

I have developed a theory that all humans need to rebel in order to become their own person, which makes my experience rather normal.

God:
Yes.

Rabbi:
You know, sometimes I do not know why I have you for a friend, you never say anything. And when you do it is terse.

God:
Yes.

Rabbi:

The main thing about my mother was that she centered her life on having four children and could never get over the fence of their importance in her life.

She would never ask if I could fix her gardens, her plumbing, all her home projects. She just assumed that I would or could do whatever she asked.
Funny thing; Patricia, my friend for over thirty years, did the very same thing. Patricia would do exactly what my mother did, she would just tell me what she wanted done and I would magically do it.

But, let me tell you, neither Patricia nor my mother knew who I was, actually. The only thing important to them was that I fell into a pattern of being their, 'home improvement guy'. Never did either of them ask about my college, my publishing, my profession as a CPA. The just took and never gave back to me.

God:
How do you think I feel about all the humans I have given so much to, and gotten so little back.

Rabbi:
Yeah, but you had them all killed, eventually.

God:
That was my job as God. Sometimes it feels good. What is your job toward your mother and her memory?

Day Twenty With God

Rabbi:
You are god yet you deserve secondary praise for allowing Beethoven to exist.

God:
Yep.

Rabbi:
His string quartets establish him as the new voice of Viennese aristocracy.

God:
I agree.

Rabbi:
To the first string quartet in F Opus 18 No 1 Allegro Con Brio, the first movement, he starts his ascent to pass Haydn and Mozart in the fast lane of music greatness.

Oh my Beethoven light as whistling willows swaying
Heavy as snow released out of mechanics of frieze
Quiet as points of melodic suspension star studded
Take me please, to your canyons of splendor, speak
Of no time or meanings but the elevation of new worlds

Oh my heart friend talking of insular understandings
Through your music I cling to warmth of your soul
I become overjoyed so thankful to hear you speak

Pilgrims of innocence heralded by invitation to
'Your majesty', we bow in reverence to your magic

Let all other praise fall from cloud burst sunshine
Give up the whisper of wind singling leaf astir
Take away that stillness of canopied shadows
Along distinct paths opening to your language
Music of preservation settling unheralded spaces

God:
Are you quite finished? Nicely done.

Day Twenty-one With God

God:
You are up late.

Rabbi:
I am fixing the electrical receptacle in the bathroom ceiling fan.
Do you have electricity in heaven?

God:
Come on! What do you think?

Rabbi:
I have no idea. I'm asking.

God:
I snap my finger for light.

Rabbi:
Well, aren't we just lucky! The wiring in my home is 110 Volt to
all the outlets and appliances except for the stove and electric
dryer. Those two items are 220 Volt.

God:
(Sarcastically)**Good thing you are not in Europe. Say, do you
know how many angels it takes to change a light bulb in
heaven? It takes twenty five thousand to turn the heavens and
one to hold the bulb.**

Rabbi:

I cannot believe how silly and simplistic you are. Here we have Muslims fighting Christians, Protestants fighting Irish Catholics and so many religions opposing each other while you tell a stupid joke.

God:

Where is it written that I have to be serious all the time?

Rabbi:

I installed the fan/light in my bathroom a year ago and the bulb receptacle broke down, but, I am so pleased that the part unscrewed and I will pay a few bucks to replace it.

God:

You want me to throw a lightning bolt down and cause you more trouble?

Rabbi:

No! Leave me alone. Go bother someone in Europe where everything is 220 volts.

God:

You know, the Europeans have had so many more years of wars and upheaval that they are more conditioned to stress than you soft-bellied Americans. You know what Oscar Wilde said about you? He said that America was the only country that went from barbarism to decadence without civilization in between.

Rabbi:

That is so unfair. There are many redeeming intellectuals and creative inventions that can be attributed to us. Like, we invented the windshield wiper

I am reading that we humans are beginning to rid ourselves of wars. The book postulates that deaths, per thousands, are lowering. But, I am caustic about over population and dwindling natural resources as well as pollution preparing the earth for a cataclysm. Is there life on other planets?

God:
Can't say.

Rabbi:
Can't or won't.

God:
Just keep buying the yearly almanac from the grocery store and wait for your answer.

Rabbi:
You are no fun.

Day Twenty-two With God

Rabbi:
I have counted time collected
for treat or tested memories.
Watched morning come and go
washing itself into night's dour.

Let this little piece of you
dissolve as sugar sadness.
Before that aged discontent
sweps me under its miseries.

I have let the pasts collide
shaking loose my reverie.
Awoken to find love entangled
with so much responsibility.

But late my knees creak,
fingers lose handiness.
And when I catch your pity
less admiration in your smile.

I dig deeper into my solace
hoping death finds my plea.

God:
I find you at your finest writing poetry.

Day Twenty-three With God

Rabbi:
In a funk unwound blues
Shoes kicked off, t-shirt
Rumpled pants and tears
Keep coming down free
Cause she went away

O how I got funk, hear me
She took all she could shove in her hatchback
She told me that she had no mind to talk

O how I got the blues
Cat watching from couch
Phone has gone cold dead
Lights are dimming
Everything is blurry

We start with love like a horse at the gun
We put all our faith in fidelity
Where is the cough syrup?
Where are the aspirins?
Give me an Ace Bandage to wrap my head
Give me a church full of holy people
Every one feeling sorry for me
I am the first man in the world who has been jilted

I am walking
Like a duck

Looking
For a lady duck
Wagging my feathers
That is the way it is with the blues

O, my grandmother warned me
She said, keep out the water if you can't swim
Keep out the kitchen if you don't know how to cook

My daddy just turned away and ma followed him
The road is empty
Car got no gas
I got the blues like a slide guitar
like a washboard and honking horn

Tomorrow came this morning
I was sad to see the day turn over
like a pancake done on both sides
I got the cow bell blues

God:
Do you expect me to react to this silliness?

Rabbi:
If the grass turns brown
Moon will always be white
Sun makes yellow smiles
Flowers sing a hungry song
Any time you need me
I will be there to ease your pain

If the night turns sour
Days crush your heart
I will be there to wish your blues away
I will be your guardian angel of joy
Tomorrow will be eager to meet up with today
You will feel just fine with my arms around you
When sorrow can't be shaken
When bright skies can't be waken
I'll be there to make it right

I've been abandoned
Been lost in this circus
Times when I was blind
No kindness could I find
But I will clear a path
To your door when you need me

Wind traces my smile to yours
Ran washes all my fears away
Smell of grass forests wake
to the ancient memories of love
I will be there all time erased
just to wipe your tears away

Little bells ring in my ears
My hair stands on end
My eyes open to new days
I ain't lonely when I am with you
Surprise at seasons changing
Wishing for promises from stars
Awake like blinking million miles

Bringing me closer hand-to-hand with you

God:
Nice!

Day Twenty-four With God

God:
You spend a lot of time listening to music.

Rabbi:
And, reading and writing.

You know the music of liturgy? My two favorite pieces are
Tchaikovsky Liturgy of St John Chrysostom, And, Rachmaninoff
Vespers. This music is a lot like polyphony or chanting. There is
something so sacred in hearing it. Ecclesiastical responsorial
chanting?

Holy, in heaven's mystery
We pray for your intercession
Giving us some small indication
Of your vast unmeasurable presence

We open our hearts to song
With overlapping melodies
Giving announcement to your power
We are but blind, wandering a desert of your gifts
Unable to find peace of heart, we beg you for salvation

God of forest, ocean, spaces of wasted emptiness
Where stillness of air envelopes us in arid magnificence

God:
Nice, very nice.

Day Twenty-five With God

Rabbi:
Thank you for always being here when I write. Do you have other things to tend to?

God:
Lots of things.

Rabbi:
How do you do that?

God:
Omnipresence. "The rocky bowels of the unsearched out depths are full of God where the sea roars, or where the solid granite leaves no interslice or vacuum, even there is God, not only in the open place, and in the chasm, but penetrating all matter, and abounding everywhere in all, and filling all things with himself."

Rabbi:
I am going to tell you something. In defining who you are, writers throughout history have come up with some of the most poetic words ever written.

God:
सर्वं खल्विदं ब्रह्म तज्जलानिति शान्त उपासीत अथ खलु क्रतुमयः पुरुषो यथाक्रतुरस्मिल्लोके पुरुषो भवति तथेतः प्रेत्य भवति स क्रतुं कुर्वीतः । Chandogya Upanishad.

"From him do all things originate, into him do they dissolve and by him are they sustained. On him should one meditate in tranquility. For as is one's faith, such indeed one is, and as is one's faith in this world, such one becomes on departing hence. Let one, therefore, cultivate faith."

Rabbi:
You are found among rocks
between each granule of
burnished desert sand.

You have come-and-gone
before and after each
sense of words
spilled from
mouths of
poets and
fools.

You are the word become blood.
Because of you there is: one
after all other numbers ...

Come together in solitude.
Stare into vastness.
At vanishing points
you will find me
stretched over
hoops of light.

Day Twenty-six With God

Rabbi:
Are you awake?

God:
Are you?

Rabbi:
I have been thinking. Please do not interrupt me till I ask.
You are God, I do not believe you have an overall plan for life. I
truly believe you simply threw the dice and what came up
doesn't mean a whole lot to you.

I do not infer but I state emphatically that you love all of your
creation. You love not what you can understand, but what you
do not understand, and that is your game: to love whatever
comes up: "seven or eleven", daddy needs a new pair of shoes.

God:
You are funny.

Rabbi:
The whole game with you is "free will" as an answer to: You not
interfering with what pops up on the dice. I get it. I and all of
your creation does what they want to do and they benefit, by
their choices, but never lose because we are eternal and can
keep doing it over-and-over till we get it right..

It is so upsetting to me that the very ground I walk upon is not real and, If I chose, I can step off into eternity and float. I may as well be a hamster for all you care, in a cage.

God:
So, what do you want? A star on your forehead? Mr. Hamster.

Rabbi:
Go to hell. I have a question.

God:
That is all you ever have - questions. Please go ahead and ask.

Rabbi:
At which point does self-confidence bleed over into false ego?

God:
All my creation. Each separate consciousness. Each single soul, either by itself or part of: What you like to call: "The great big mixed up gestalt. All of you individually or as a whole, take responsibility for knowing when you are correct or overblown egotistically.

Tell me. What is the real reason you are confused on this issue?

Rabbi:
There is a woman who thinks she knows me and I am feigning indifference to her because I really am not interested in her.

God:

Here we go! Always it boils down to the uncertainty of. the sexes.

"So you ride yourself all over the fields.

And you make all your animal deals

andyour wise men do not know how it feels,

to be thick as a brick."

Day Twenty-seven With God

God:
Do not be afraid. I am here with you.

Rabbi:
It was an abrupt wake up. My feet were cold. I urinated and totally forgot what the dream was.

God:
I know.

Rabbi:
The dream was short and very intense. It involved me interacting with another person. It was not a depressive interaction.

God:
Take your mind off of it for now. Remember, dreams come from our need to touch our deeper self.

Rabbi:
Do you dream?

God:
Why would you even think that I do not dream? Of course I do.

Rabbi:
What do you dream about?

God:

That, is not for you to know.   You are distracting the attention away from your feelings and your dream.

Rabbi:

My dream is the filigree filament

It floats out of sight like a scarred rabbit

When mind-over-matter comes front-and-center

My dream would hurt you with its essence of innocence

I come upon a disturbance as wishes become reality

And, I let invisible angels comfort me with forgetting

Day Twenty-eight With God

Rabbi:
Save it for the psychologist
the emperor has no clothes

oh would some power give us
to see ourselves as others see us

there are three people:
1)who we think we are
2)who others think we are
3)who some outside spirit force knows us in truth

whenever I feel insecure, I think of my ex-spouse and how she
still hates me after forty years of being divorced

most people think they are victims
I try to take what is dealt me and turn it into activism

when someone calls me a fool, I double it

it is so easy to be a fool, but hard to learn from it

I love Shakespeare for many things, mainly: A rose is a rose,
by any other name is still a rose - thus: I am who I am,
by any other who

the right hand never knows what the left is doing

If someone tells you they believe in a god they have never seen, then give them a mirror

I classify gods as more powerful than me because they have learned to be invisible
I appreciate all beauty in the world then I imagine it all being taken away by someone who resembles evil

if I am to suffer in hell than I will suffer, more so, in heaven

if a door is locked, than go around it

I danced till I was exhausted then slept till I woke refreshed

my heart is so full of regrets that I cut it out so now I am heartless and now where my heart used to be is an empty place for love

I get so tired of people telling me to have a good day that I squirt them with water and elicit surprise out of them

my feeling of being hungry is really a misplaced insecurity that I am not hungry, only thinking it

I could never live with another person because they will never get over all the incessant habits I engage in to avoid my loneliness

if you say you love me then save it for the psychologist who gets paid for hearing it

Day Twenty-nine With God

Rabbi:
I write these series with God for my next book. Book number fourteen; for sale at Amazon.

I do not write this series for comments. In fact, not one poet on the site - All Poetry - comes close to critiquing my work. I am my best commentator.

When I write, I first want to say something. Next I use poetic device. In other words, I write for effect. I write a sonnet and invariably, a contest holder criticizes my meter scheme. I write a sonnet to make a point and that point has nothing to do with iambic pentameter or rhyme. The most prominent aspect of my writing is the sound of the words placed in a poem or writing. If something sounds good to my ear, I then work to make the sound fit poetic structures.

One of my favorite writers is Carl Sandburg, for his plain talk.

God:
"Oh Lord, please don' let me be misunderstood
Yes, I'm just a soul whose intentions are good."

Rabbi:
There will always be misunderstanding. It's the way of things, because no two people have the same thought process. Just like no two snowflakes are similar.

I do not mean to hurt other people's feelings, but I know how good a writer I am and I know how bad a writer I am, so, I keep stabbing the beast till I am satisfied that I am expressing myself as best as possible.

Day Thirty With God

God:
What's up?

Rabbi:
I have a premonition
Of how our world will end
With tears and lamentation
When souls and matter blend
Our hearts in deep suspension
Our minds in silence lend
Themselves to recognition
Of prayers that we must tend

God:
Hmm!

Rabbi:
Often we pray only when we are desperate
feeling sad or lost. We turn back to humility
when life has humbled us into submission.
We often forget that all peoples on earth
are, necessarily, faulted. None of us is perfect.
Are you perfect?

God:
Hell no!

Rabbi:
Our religions want you to exemplify perfection.

God:
I know. And that is your religious fallacy.

Rabbi:
But, we need a supreme goal.

God:
Life is not a football game.
Look inside your heart for perfection.

Rabbi:
Dear Lord, I love and honor you above all things.

God:
Go love your cat. Nature is a form of perfection.

Rabbi:
Tornadoes, hurricanes, pole shifts, earthquakes, wars - what the hell are you talking about?

God:
The only thing constant in the universe is change.

Rabbi:
I am going to find an island of perfect temperature with no dictators or evil, and live forever.

God:
Good luck. Let me know when you do.

Day Thirty-one With God

God:
Hey!

Rabbi:
Hey, yourself.

God:
Sibelius?

Rabbi:
Yea. His music ascends to joyfulness
When little spaces of notes catch onto us like stars
Dropping out of a peaceful night sky going into new orbits.

Drinking warm tea spiced with rum
Feet warm in wool socks on the wood floor
Sibelius brings nationalism to heights
Like pronouncements of grandeur
Regal concentric melodies
Making us feel right at home on the edge of Gulf of Bothnia
flowing into the icy Baltic Sea.

Sibelius keeps Sweden and Estonia awake in waves of sound.
All of Helsinki eats their morning muffins to the music of their
idol.

God:
Nice.

Day Thirty-two With God

Rabbi:
I talk and talk and nobody listens
Dreams escape me, I am lost
Days come and go, I am in prison
Locked into boundaries of my own making

People say they know me, but have no clue
I do not want to be rude, but just stay away from me
I am in a chocolate mood - dark and somber

To all the clients who have cheated me out of money
God has made it up by giving me more money than I need

To all the wives who got the better of me in court
It has been made up to me by all the women whom
I did not marry

My jello hardens just right
My left over food spoils just right
My cuts and bruises heal
My hip no longer hurts without surgery
I sleep just fine
I remember people that I have loved
And pray for them in requiems
People like Virginia, like my mother,
Like all the good people

I have nothing but disdain for erratic drivers

And those who rush to get ahead of me
In the checkout lanes I head toward

I never get the blues for any length of time
Longer than it takes to change music I am listening to

I am happy believing in a god who is my pal
A God who does not judge me
A God who has heartburn and needs love

God:
Lots of love!
I need it; bushel baskets full.

Day Thirty-three With God

Rabbi:
Summer closes its season
Fall creeps in on arid leaves
Winter drops its scarf around

Shoulders of trees and burnt out gray hills
Arms extended up into columns of clouds
Embracing all magic new-born, embryonic

Of course, we wait for spring come out
Of its dormer of solace
Spring with pastels
Spring with faint colors
Mentioned with solemn references
Out of the bible of illustrated sourdough

I am prince of principalities
Drunken wastrel

My family expects too much
That I shall not succeed at
But, whores of interest
Will confirm my kindness

I am rancid with diseases
Histories will never admit to

Day Thirty-four With God

Rabbi:
Summer closes its season
Fall creeps in on arid leaves
Winter drops its scarf around

Shoulders of trees and burnt out gray hills
Arms extended up into columns of clouds
Embracing all magic new-born, embryonic

Of course, we wait for spring come out
Of its dormer of solace
Spring with pastels
Spring with faint colors
Mentioned with solemn references
Out of the bible of illustrated sourdough

I am prince of principalities
Drunken wastrel

My family expects too much
That I shall not succeed at
But, whores of interest
Will confirm my kindness

I am rancid with diseases
Histories will never admit to

Day Thirty-five With God

God:
Something's troubling you?

Rabbi:
There are things I do not tell you.
There are things I do not tell my doctor.

God:
Oh boy, here we go. Like, I need you to tell me.

Rabbi:
All people keep many things to themselves and they die without ever revealing them.

Caesar kept his fears to himself and died forgetting to shake the hand of Brutus.
Henry the II wanted to hug his son, Richard, even when the sword went through his belly.
What the hell would Ernest Hemingway have told us before he pulled the trigger on his shotgun?

You know, you are God and there are so many things you never tell us humans, even to the point where we die.

God:
I tell you everything you need to know.

Rabbi:

Oh! Great! Thanks for the distinction of giving us just what you think is good for us.

I will tell you why I refrain from revealing all things to my doctor. You see, he does not need to know how I am able to cure myself of most things that I do not need to bother him about.

God:

Is there a difference between that and me knowing that humanity will figure most things out for themselves?

Rabbi:

I guess not. But I will tell you this: Humanity is delusional as well as me. We think we have things figured out, but I will tell you what Milt Weidmeyer told me years ago: He said, "Rabbi, we CPA's make all these provisions for estate planning and when the client dies, we are faced with a problem that we did not think of."

You know, God, when we paint the side of the barn we stand back with pride, yet as years pass, there is one spot where the paint begins to peel and we know that we painted that spot, but there is life: In a few years the whole barn will begin to fade from that one spot outward.

I have peace in my soul, but there are misgivings in my heart over your presence in my dreams. You are an unknown quantity in my life and death and when I talk to you, even now, you do not really have all the facts on me.

God:
I have all the facts I need on you.
Rabbi:
Arrogant bastard ....
God:
Watch it............... I can be testy, too.

Rabbi:
You watch it.

God:
What is it you did not tell your doctor?

Rabbi:
Doesn't matter. Even if I tell him, he would stand on his soap box and tell me: "I told you so."

Everybody takes the high road and says: "I told you so."

It is as if people want to be self-righteous and lie to the world that they knew things would turn out just the way they envisioned them.

I am going to end this little tete-a-tete with you and say I know how your Godship will end. You will be forgotten in a world of computers and robots.

God:
You're probably right.

So what?

Day Thirty Six With God

Rabbi:
Our spirit searches fulfillment
Inner strength of confidence
Never reaching completeness
Advancing toward nirvana
Placated by false assumptions
We settle for love. You laugh?

God:
I seek what you seek.

Rabbi:
We pretend that we please you
But deep, we envy your singularity

My god! You are god!
You're perfection.

God:
Your mythology, not mine.

Rabbi:
Every species on this planet has created a god to believe in.

God:
Your mythology, not mine.

Rabbi:
Sometimes I hate you.
God:
Your mythology, not mine.

Rabbi:
If you are telling me that you are imperfect, then we have nothing to believe in.

God:
Your mythology, not ...

Rabbi:
I heard you! ...

Day Thirty Seven With God

Rabbi:
Remember smoke where shells landed
Stark reminders of death swirling all about
Gut stretched taut from resolution of fear

My uncle's words coming back to me:
"Why should I worry about him when I have seen real men,
better than him, get their heads blown off right next to me."

There are more important things to worry about
When death is near
We worry about if we peed our pants
We worry if we are bleeding
We worry about if we can get a message to our mother
Dear mother still recovering from birthing us
She, worrying about if her son is alive

I am a silent winged prayer
Thinking holiness when tracer rounds
Are zig-zagging erratically as if an etch-a-sketch
Or fireworks innocently mimicking a
Real fire fight

I worry about the screams of Coghenour, Besse,
Slack crying out in vain to a merciless god who is
Extinguishing them willy-nilly like church candles going out

God:
I heard them.

Rabbi:
Take me into your arms
Secure my safety

God:
I hear you.

Rabbi:
The terror as if some monster indefinable will eat us alive.

God:
I hear you.

Rabbi:
I close my eyes and let sound pass through my ears
I fondle my rifle wood butt end stock as if it is a crucifix
I count my fingers to verify that my mind is working
It is a crucible of faith that I let go and place my trust in God

Day Thirty Eight With God

Rabbi:
I am sole survivor
evolution in motion

Why does corned beef, sauerkraut, mustard taste so good?

Maggie died at age ninety four
A greasy hamburger, fries, beer out of a frosted glass
I sat and watched her eat like she was a Montessori pupil

Maggie was my friend for over forty years
Before she died, she denounced me
Cause, she had lost her mind
I guess when she got to heaven
She remembered what she forgot

God:
Maybe.

Rabbi:
Norm died
We were the only two people who went to his funeral
He was a miser
He was buried in the same pants he never changed
Before he died, Maggie and myself took him to lunch
For his last birthday, he asked for the toilet paper
That we used to buy for him every year

Maggie really got mad at me - during Norms funeral,
I waved a five dollar bill over his sewed up lips and chalky face.
He never moved in the coffin

I told Maggie that maybe that was how Jesus brought
Lazarus back from the dead

God:
You are silly.

Rabbi:
No, you are silly for how you take us away from life.

God:
I do my job well.

Rabbi:
You know, Lazarus told Jesus that now, he had to die all over
again.

God:
So? I did my job for Lazarus twice.

Day Thirty Nine With God

Rabbi:

I am colored crayon chalk lines cutting into topical seizures

Only a bird can touch my wings

Ever a sonnet of serious language

Come close my heart is elusive

When light opened a heaven

The brilliance shone through

Filigree filament prospered

All is awoken in a burst of space

Worms came forth

Trees spun roots

Whatever was imagined

Was beside itself in prominence

Stand back force yourself to solitude

I will hold you into view forever

God:

Nice.

Day Forty With God

Rabbi:
(I'm) Confused over Octavia Paz and his general theme of male seclusion.
Confused how he classes women as passive exclusively.
How he structures society as individuals who never open their hearts to any truth as a defensive mechanism. He claims revealing their intimate thoughts make them vulnerable.

God:
Yea?

Rabbi:
I will tell you this: Paz leads to a new world with the end of World War II and with Aleksandr Solzhenitsyn's famous exposition of Stalin and his death camps. Civilization goes from barbarism, to dark ages, to Medieval, to Renaissance, to industrial revolution with its world wars, and now, the computer age.

God:
Yea?

Rabbi:
I get lost as to what is important in our new world of information age.
Seems like all humanity is backed against the wall of wanting to know everything and therefore cannot pin point anything important.

We are like the end of the Roman Empire which got lost in wanting to know quickly without meaning whatsoever.

God:
Yes.

Rabbi:
You are not much help.

God:
(Smiling) **I do my best.**

Rabbi:
You know current thinking is that the world will be controlled totally in the near future by artificial intelligence. And, as I warned you, it probably will mean the end of all gods replaced by robots.

God:
I hear you.

Rabbi:
The robots will envision their own god, and you will be forgotten.

I think you and I both should find a secluded island and build our huts across from each other.

God:
Just don't take my newspaper in the morning.

Day Forty One With God

God:
What's Up?

Rabbi:
Same old, same old.
Say, how do you keep track of all the souls alive and dead?

God:
Wouldn't you like to know!

Rabbi:
Stephen Hawking says that we are very close to understanding God.

God:
As I am close to understanding Steven Hawking. Believe half of what you see and nothing of what you hear.

Rabbi:
Look, I will tell you this: What difference is there if we understand you completely, since you are not going to reverse the mixed up mess we got ourselves into on this planet.

We created it and we will solve it.

I have often wondered about god - you - and I have come to realize that it is waste of time. First of all, you never give humanity answers.

God:
I give signals.

Rabbi:
Oh, you wave semaphore flags?
Morse code? Telegraph?

I, personally, do not really like Stephen Hawking. His attitude is
so superior and aloof.   Whether you will be revealed or
whether you stay circumspect, I adore you for all the beauty that
does not get destroyed by bible burners or assholes.

Nobody on this earth can recreate the absolute beauty of a pear
cut in half, or a winter snow storm. You are an enigma and a
genius.

Say, do you really hear all the prayers that people pray for?

God:
You tell me. Are your prayers answered?

Rabbi:
I ain't won the lotto yet.

God:
(Smiling broadly) **If you do, I can give you a good CPA.**

Rabbi:
I am a CPA,
 no thanks.

Day Forty Two With God

Rabbi:
Gods and angels listen to my story
Merciless words that give no glory

Where have meadows disappeared?
Song of blackbirds no longer heard

Gods and angels listen to my story
Why does night not wake refreshed
Breath of dew gets tangled in trash
Cities stumble on edges of tin cans
Plastic shred bags caught on fences
Papers contracted in mud dried hard

Humanity dangles at edge of doom
Broken glass, plastic scattered ruin

How highest buildings rise to extinction
How low we gaze into cracked streets
When spring comes between crevices
Stubborn weeds give us messages
False sun flowers rehearsing grays

Gods and angels where does it end
Sorrows of bleached broken windows
Deep regret stretched empty houses
Colors diminished trees broken limbs

Where does it stop give our eyes rest?
In empty churches no longer blessed
See children's playthings all faded
Schools boarded students graded
To their futures exchanged despair

I am going to the highest fence
Look over to see if hope is alive
And I see lines of exhausted cars
No longer able to start or drive.

What can we do with fallen wires?
Leaning telephone poles
Deaf to a silence
Like my words
Becoming
Senseless.

God:
Nicely done!

Day Forty Three With God

Rabbi:
I come from a family that has no history of suicides.
We are all too stubborn or afraid, not sure why.
Of course, you maybe can count Uncle Mike
who drank himself to death, non-stop.
All the rest waited patiently for old age
or death to get the upper hand.

I, personally, conjecture that I do not have high cholesterol and
my doctor always gives me a pat on the back for reaching the
eighties.

I cannot complain, you see there have been times when I got
close to passing through the veil, but I chose to remain on this
side because there were too many things cementing me here.
Three times, but I will leave them in the grab bag of silence.

There is a certain self-satisfaction in outliving some of the
people who I did not care too much about. But, I cannot gloat
'cause they are dead and non-communicative ... And I will soon
be joining them.

Like, my uncle George, who whispered into my ear at a wedding:
"You are doing good. We got our eye on you." He is dead, but I
am not sure he knew anything about me at all; except that I was
his brother's first born. He died rich, an ex-gangster - wife and
two children crying for him.

The list of suicides is long: Virginia Wolf, Ernest Hemingway, Marc Antony, Cleopatra, William Kotzwinkle (who was a writer from San Francisco). So many people who were not brave enough to face life squarely.

Suicides are, generously, put to sleep for as long as it takes for them to be woken and apprised of their decision to try to kill themselves. Then they are informed that they must be reborn and recreate the explicit circumstances that they succumbed to, in their prior life, and defeat those circumstances in their reincarnated life.

Sort of makes it a waste of time to commit suicide.

Most of the people in my family were immigrants from the old country and to talk to them about suicide or academics would be like talking to a cat that has fallen asleep on your lap.

God:
Where is all this talk going? What's the point?

Rabbi:
You are God, be patient. Have you ever thought of suicide?

God:
Never, *(smiles)* except when I get tired of your talking so much.

Day Forty Four With God

Rabbi:
A Sonnet To Love

Intemperate availing thyself of time
Looking not for flowering bidden lies
Wantonness, poetry keeps us blind
Waiting impatiently is its own prize

O how nature structured, it implies
Fairness in balancing all with trust
That form will cover all that complies
With content satisfying love for lust

But, I am genuine, given perchance
Small space inside your secretness
Words greater than a heavy lance
Will win you over in your sacredness

Fear not dispel all your bad dreams
For lust will lose all that love deems

God:
Nice.

Day Forty Five With God

Rabbi:
We are not desert bugs
Searching food, water
Surprised while bats eat us
Atop frozen heights,
Kazakhstan snow leopards dwindling
In tree tops Brazilian rain forest
Spider monkeys surviving
limb-to-branch-to-limb
You and me are homo sapiens
Tracing ourselves back to caves in
Xuchang Henan province
Chinese Denisovan neighbors
We are ancient ancients of
Unheralded obscurity
Secluded histories
Non heroic
Bleached bones
Vacuous
Skulls

God:
Go on, go on ...

Rabbi:
I am tired.

Day Forty Six With God

Rabbi:

I am beginning to see my life as an abstract.
Nothing is real anymore. Everything has jagged edges that
scrape and I no longer can fit those things into the portfolio of
my history.

When I drive my car, it is as if I am riding atop of an elephant. I
make wrong turns and, at times, I get out and stop cars passing
me. I ask their drivers if they know where they are going.
Mostly, they dial 911 to get the cops after me. I get out of there
real fast.

I usually park behind the mall and urinate on my feet,
accidentally. It is real strange because I no longer can aim my
urine effectively and it goes everywhere. There is not much I
can do to avoid me scattering. I prefer to defecate because it
plops straight down into the toilet. I do not defecate out doors
or in strange bathrooms. I can only defecate in my toilet. If I am
shopping, I hold it in till I get home.

I no longer have a cat. Cats do not live as long as I would like
them to live. They die. I have to bury them in secret places in
respect to their wishes. Not one of my cats has had a laying out.
I always wrap their dead bodies in a very clean towel - terry
cloth - and I put them in a shoe box. The places where those
shoe boxes are buried are quiet places that will not be dug up
any-too-soon. I keep my cat graves alive in my memory and, at
times, I pray to the spot where they are buried.

Where George is buried, I visit with flowers. I always piss behind George's grave in deference to his wishes. George's headstone is metal, flat and his name is on the left and his wife's name on the right. I never pray to her, only to him. She was not like him. She was strange in that she always fainted when visitors gave George too much attention. Her name was Martha, but that doesn't matter. When she faked fainting, George would wave his hand and tell people to not get excited, that she would recover in a few minutes. That would infuriate Martha and she would ask for a cold towel that she kept patting her forehead with, as if the compress helped her get her senses back. Funny thing about Martha was she always wore boxy shoes with huge back heels so she could get good footing. Her heels were like horseshoes - Clydesdale.

I do not want to concentrate on Martha, but I will tell you this - the grave plate, with her name on the right and his on the left, had a small hollowed out holder to put flowers in between their names. If I brought flowers for George, I would put them in that holder with some water and then I would bend the flowers gently toward his name so that she would not get the benefit of the flowers.

Sometimes I would not be able to buy flowers when I visited him, so I would steal flowers from another grave and use them for George.

My life has begun to not be real to me. Lately I have been forgetting what day it is and I do not believe my cell phone, but I go shopping and I will ask Dana or Annie what day it is. I always apologize to them and tell them that it feels like Sunday, even when it only feels like a Friday. It is a lot easier to lie to Dana or Annie, since they really do not care whether it is Christmas or Labor Day. They are nice people. Annie is married and Dana doesn't know. I like Annie for pretending that she is my wife and I like Dana to pretend that I divorced her but kept good relations with her. I, of course, never tell them, but I buy each of them candy and put the receipt in the bag so they do not get questioned by their supervisor.

Dana is very tall and voluptuous. Annie is a short hunch back person with a charitable manner about her. She always looks upset but maintains her smile if anyone bumps her or greets her.

Annie's hair is disheveled, Dana's hair is comfit-ed or short and in place. Dana's hair is black like black. Annie's hair is like a golden retriever's.

I apologize for spending too much time on these two persons, but they are my favorite.

I am not ready yet for assisted living or a nursing home. I feel like I will not go home someday, but go to a nursing home and find an empty room, close the door and go to sleep. Of course I will take a meal tray off of the cart, in the morning and switch the name tag onto a used up eaten tray.

God:
You are a total wacko!

Day Forty Seven With God

Rabbi:
If you cover yourself with pride
You will freeze to death.

Excerpt:

The Iliad, Book I, Lines 1-15

RAGE:
Sing, Goddess, Achilles' rage,
Black and murderous, that cost the Greeks
Incalculable pain, pitched countless souls
Of heroes into Hades' dark,
And left their bodies to rot as feasts
For dogs and birds, as Zeus' will was done.
Begin with the clash between Agamemnon--
The Greek warlord--and godlike Achilles.

Which of the immortals set these two
At each other's throats?

Apollo, Zeus' son and Leto's, offended
By the warlord. Agamemnon had dishonored
Chryses, Apollo's priest, so the god
Struck the Greek camp with plague,
And the soldiers were dying of it.

Rabbi:

So, in the first book of history, Achilles pride over being offended by Agamemnon, causes untold pain on the Greeks.

How much do we need to understand that pride or ego is our biggest problem on this earth?

Ego of all great leaders and people we call wise, ego is their blind-spot. We have road rage. We have prideful people taking guns into their hands to hurt other people.

Ego filled distorted Hitler, Stalin. They believed they were better than the people they killed. They never prayed or cared for the millions that they froze to death, burned to death, starved to death. For one moment of sanity to see themselves in reality, they spent all their moments on earth believing in a demon in their hearts. We have teachers and leaders full of themselves to all else excluded.

Buddha teaches us to meditate till we are empty and then the true spirit will come into our hearts.

God:
Buddha is our master ...

Day Forty Eight With God

Rabbi:
I have a heart full of indecision
Mind just released from prison

Sorrow laden shoulders dread
Discussions made in my head

Alone and clever not lonely
Stupid and call myself loony

Reading, thinking less human
Cross referencing with acumen

I believe all religions are valid
Like a slavering dog so rabid

I try to be nice to stupid souls
Surprised what little they know

But do not get me wrong
Sing off-key a sad song

My life is a grain of salt
My drink is a stout malt

My eyes brown hide deep
Thoughts I should not keep

But to you I would never lie
Not afraid to laugh or cry

God:
You make couplets easily.

Day Forty Nine With God

Rabbi:

My sister, Anita, wants me to behave to her satisfaction. I am not cruel to her, but simply continue to act in my manner. She wants me to have dialogue with her friend and I am not interested.

Not sure what to do other than ignoring her.

I refuse to have conversation with someone that I share no common ground with. If you think you know me, then you are much smarter than me, because I work hard at trying to know who I am, and I rarely come close to the truth of me. I am a graduated idiot. I am an ungrateful recipient of dishonor.

Frances Mary Louise DePonio, ran into me in a parking lot in Ann Arbor Michigan. She asked if she could come over my house and talk. I thanked her and declined. I did not remind her that she married and divorced without me being involved. She did say these exact words to me: "I like the man you have become." I said to her, quietly, "I also like the man I have become." She never came to my house and that was the last I heard from her.

My sister, Anita, calls me continuously to read poems she has written, and I listen but never comment to her. I do tell her that her poems are good and she tells me how the people in her poetry meeting group, love her work. I do not know how to avoid delusions. That is her business. But, I cannot and never will be delusional, if I can avoid it. I am the worst writer and most singular person I know. I will go to hell or heaven depending on the spin of the bottle. I will accept the hemlock and drink it if you do not like me.

God:
Would you be willing to substitute arsenic or strychnine?

Rabbi:
As long as they work; I do not want to survive a botched poisoning.

Day Fifty With God

Interlude
- excerpt or quote from Viktor Frankl 03-26-1905 to 09-02-1997
When we are no longer able to change a situation, we are challenged to change ourselves.
Between stimulus and response there is a space. In that space is our power to choose our response. In our response lies our growth and our freedom.
Everything can be taken from a man but one thing: the last of the human freedoms—to choose one's attitude in any given set of circumstances, to choose one's own way.

Rabbi:
I am not a Rabbi. I am a dissident Rabbi. I bless or kosher pork, rosaries or front wheel differential axles.

My facts are that I am a full blood Rabbi with genetic links to the Phoenicians who slept with my ancestral villagers on straw in the barns of my becoming, in the mountains of my dreams.

Before electricity, my grandfather Ferris lost his barn to fire. The brigade passed buckets forward to try to extinguish it.

My grandmother fell into Louie's arms trying to save the horses with a pitchfork and pail of water.

Years later in the back room of a house in Grosse Pointe Michigan, my grandmother on my dad's side, sat with bloated ankles, a shawl covering her and her shockingly stringy gray hair, in a rocking chair beside the gas burning room stove. She held a screw cap glass bottle (Kerr Jar) that she drank warm water out of. She put white cream on her face making her resemble an old woman ghost. I used to try scraping the white thickness off her face.

She was rich and all her family waited for her to die so that they could finally get their hands on the insurance money she saved from suing (somebody) for her daughters car accident injury..

I was eight years old and she pulled me into her lap and said sternly to me: "The blood of Jesus runs through your veins."

She was not scary, but pathetic. I tried to tell her that the blood of Phoenician sailors ran through our veins and that Jesus was a Jew.

My grandmother, Zahia, would pray in Yiddish without knowing it. I was always amazed how the skin color and personality types between the Jew and the Arab, were so similar

She was horrified to causing my father to try to pull me out of her lap. She clung tight to me, then pulling me up she took me into the basement where she let me help her cook the special foods that only she knew.

I am not a Rabbi, but the name is indicative of a holy person and I try to live as a holy person of my making and not of any church or synagogue rules. By labeling myself as a Rabbi, I come with the possibilities of many kinds as opposed to a Priest being so one sided.

The last priest I came into contact with, hid under his bed during a mortar attack.

I am now reading Viktor Frankl's famous book - man's search for meaning. The main premise of the book is that meaning in life comes from the content and not the form.

Therefore, I am a contextual Rabbi and a human being in form. I do not believe but I live in my belief.

God:
(rolls eyes) **Oy vey**

Day Fifty One With God

Rabbi:
My piano

Two hands overlapping
Foot pedal diminuendo
Place where rain mutes the tight wires
Like birds my fingers hold to keys vibrating
Sending correspondent notes in melodic passion
My piano like pots-'n'-pans arranging themselves by size
Notes that spiral into concentric funnels
My piano is lustrous language of ivory keys
Letting us into their world

God:
Your piano?

Rabbi:
Deliver me birthing C minor
Dwelling in Nod, land of spaces.
My piano of what is less than more of life.
Aspiring to be a train, regular motion
An engine of deliberation
A beast of echoes
Moving right
Into night.

God:
(shakes head)

Day Fifty Two With God

Rabbi:
Reading of men digging tunnels in World War One.
Trenches beneath enemy lines.
When they caved in, the men suffocated.

I had to stop reading that book.

I am now reading of concentration camp conditions and the reality of mental breaks in the prisoners at different stages. A book laced with constant death surrounding the survivors who stayed alive doing unbearable hard tasks in extreme weather conditions with no shoes or clothes protecting them whatsoever.

I am half way through this book and I fear I will have to give it up because I am not able to place this reality into my mind.

We, born after World War II, even if we served in Vietnam, as I did, we never had to endure the inquisition or slavery, or death camps of Stalin or Hitler. There is a collection of torture stories that chill the mind, such as impalement or death with a pole driven through the body. Stories of death on the wheel or the rack. Death by small cuts into the body slowly letting the victim keep awake while bleeding to death. Crucifixion being one of the most painful ways to die.

We are soft people who float in and out of experience, mostly in comfort. We maintain medicines and wool sheets while we keep our minds free of realities of disinherited peoples who suffer from hunger or disease. To us, those peoples live in places we imagine do not even exist. We deny their pain by not thinking about it.

I am not a brave person and I have never been tested by injustice.

God:
Nor, do you ever want to be.

Rabbi:
Why am I so lucky?

God:
It is not luck. It is because this not in your learning requirement. If it was something you needed to grow deeper spiritually, then you would be given the fortitude to endure it.

Day Fifty Three With God

Rabbi:
I am covered over with eternity
Blanket of protection sunless night
Beside streaming stars comforted
Knowing existences beyond my understanding
Keep me humble as a rabbit laying still for danger

Call to books of memories
Let loose the library of volumes
Holy psalms and prayers
Pages of progression
Each one a lesson
Overcoming
Sadness
Mostly

Delicate wrinkles
Ironed out to fit with other pages
Move ribbon bookmark and my pride
Reaching peace within this short time
As love fills in the cavities of restlessness

God:
You are at your best here.

Day Fifty Four With God

Rabbi:
I collect myself into emotion years ago
Did I do anything wrong to the neighbor lady?
I had several dinners with her and on one visit to my apartment;
she brought her two grandchildren of two and three years old.
I handed the children books to possibly read.
When they begin to rip the pages out of the books, I told the
lady to leave the children alone, the books did not matter.
In time the children begin to mimic me reading from my book,
and they begin to do the same.

I had not gotten intimate with that women, but the weekend
after the children, the lady invited me over for dinner. When I
opened the door to her apartment I saw that she had incense,
candlelight and a lovely meal spread out, and I knew she was
upping the relationship to falling in love with me.

Now, my reaction at her door was immediate. I turned around
and never saw her again.

It was a decisive moment and I have never regretted it.
It was that I was not worthy of being her mate, but I was
absolutely not ready. I had spent the last few years praying for a
spiritual adviser who had not been given to me.

It took another three years until my prayers were answered and
for thirty five years that adviser guided my life the way I wanted
it.

I am a red blooded man who loves women, but I never regretted being celibate for one main reason: relationships of a personal nature are very time consuming and demanding. I was in need of solitude and much work on my spiritual centers, which worked out to be just what I did for all this time. I am not a perfect rabbi but I am happy and I have reached this point without taking up the time and effort of a wife or mate.

God:
(melodramatically) **I have heard your story over and over ...**

Rabbi:
Alright, I will shut up.

Day Fifty Five With God

Interlude:
Martin Luther King Jr. "A Descending Spiral"
"The ultimate weakness of violence is that it is a descending
spiral, begetting the very thing it seeks to destroy. Instead of
diminishing evil, it multiplies it. Through violence you may
murder the liar, but you cannot murder the lie, nor establish the
truth. Through violence, you may murder the hater, but you do
not murder hate. In fact, violence merely increases hate. So it
goes. Returning violence for violence multiplies violence, adding
deeper darkness to a night already devoid of stars. Darkness
cannot drive out darkness: Only light can do that. Hate cannot
drive out hate: Only love can do that."

Rabbi:
We often forget how magical words were put together by wise
men.

God:
Souls I am very proud of.

Rabbi:
My descending spiral.

We cannot stop the volcano of darkness.
Our actions spew ash into a dark sky and close out the sun.
It is only through our refusal to hate that we quell the explosion
of mayhem that encircles the earth.
We must let the sun into the day to keep the night in check.

Never was a time more important to love. To love in our words. To love in our actions our deeds and, ultimately, in our thoughts. Our ancestors wait, stalled in history.

They wait for our understanding to clear our path to wisdom. Civilization draw strings itself into a satchel of thoughts that grow too large to be contained, but overflow into all life's. We can and will unblock the light to life and love eternally.

God:
Nicely put.

Day Fifty Six With God

Rabbi:
Hymn 8:60. Agni. (The Rigveda)
O Agni, with thy mighty wealth guard us from all malignity.

Save us from high cholesterol.
Let not high blood pressure put us in danger of that imp of
death.

O Agni keep us free of diabetes.
Protect us from kidney deficiencies or liver deterioration.
We have taken our medicines with obedience.
Worn head cover in winter storms.
Dressed appropriately for inclement weather.
Used umbrellas.
Worn rubber boots in rain.

O Agni when we still or cast fished from the silent banks of
Colorado's winding rivers of the South Platte, Green, San Juan -
so many carved through the uplifted mountains of Rockies,
Mount Elbert and all the Sawatch range, we used only fresh bait
and new spinners, shiny lures and threw back the small fish that
deserved more time to grow large and fat for catching.

You have seen us, Agni - You the guardian of the earth - Seen us
recycle and keep your paths clear of empty cans and waste
papers. We, who have been given so many choices, pack out all
garbage responsibly.

We kept to designated paths and observed with gratitude the skunk cabbage, ferns of so many leafs leaning into moss covered mushroom families.

We have protected the beavers and groundhogs who depend upon cavities in trees and ground holes to make their homes in safety.

To Agni Jatavedas, to the son of strength, that you may give us precious gifts we give back to you all our possessions. And we pray for your eternal soul matched to our soul in love.

God:
(feigning hurt) **You mock me.**

Rabbi:
Just playing.

Day Fifty Seven With God

Rabbi:
We all are conservators of rituals.
Move the fork and knife to the right.
Put the sock on the right foot first.

My son arrives and puts his keys here, his phone there and before the visit has even begun, he has staked out so many places in my house that I watch with wonder as to why he acts as he does.

I imagine that he has to feel safe by marking his spots like a snow leopard or a brown bear.

Years ago, I took a shower in a friend's house and as I stepped onto the rug to towel off, she was brushing up against me cleaning the wall and floor of the shower, even before I was out of her way. She was so ritualistic that she had to clean immediately as if in a trance of habit that consumed her.

Jeanne said to us at breakfast. "Would you please clean your hair out of the shower drain." I was taken aback by the realization that my drained out hair accumulated to her discomfort. From that time forward, I keep the little metal drain cap free of my hair in every house I live in.

Look at the clock constantly, is a habit, I think, we all do. We judge when to eat, sleep, wake by the clock. It is a ritual I now defend instead of ridicule. It is so ingrained within us to be aware of time.

Even in the short five years I was married or in cohabitation with another person, I found myself falling into ritualistic behavior that was surprising to me.

As a bachelor for over forty years, my patterns would be stock for ridicule if any one observed. I am lucky to engage myself in private, but even I laugh at what I do to be comfortable with my solitary living condition. We can realistically say that rituals control our lives.

Let me tell you how religion is important, even if belief systems can be analyzed from derivations or customs inherited. The fervor with which we pray is separate from the form.

God:
I hear your prayers regardless of what your faith is.

Rabbi:
Do you answer the prayers of established religions faster than 'walk-on' Christians?

God:
You ask the funniest things.

Rabbi:

Painting by Vaslily Surkov"

Exiling of the Boyarina Morozova (1632-1675)

Noble lady being exiled for not following the ritual of two fingers raised as a blessing sign of the Old Believers.

I remember, as an altar boy, serving mass and assisting the priest in rituals of prayer and customs that were apart from the actual prayers. It is an old idea of "Form versus Function"

We, altar boys, would pour the water and wine into the chalice held out by the celebrant. The functionary would raise the chalice, ever so slightly, as a sign for us to stop pouring. I remember Jimmy Callaghan joking with me how he kept pouring to get the priest mad.

God:
I would be mad, too!

Rabbi:
It figures.

Day Fifty Eight With God

Rabbi:
It is Sunday I need god, my church is closed
My Mullah has no kerchief to blow his nose
Angels all sleeping not caring who knows
Rudolph now has no red shiner that glows
I have no ability to convert, its a no-show
I've a cough and gas where wind don't blow

Please help me send a dusty old janitor
With wrenches poking out of his clothes
A bandana, bib overalls old Red Wings
Mustard on his T-Shirt where food goes

I need a nurse white shoes and blouse
No sexy woman but knows how it goes

O where is my salvation at this late hour
I need a philosopher, no smile, real dour
I am telling you the truth, I have no power
To cure myself I will take a cold shower
Practice for a last judgment: I 'll cower

My horse has no saddle My car no gas
I probably need a good kick in the ass
But I will wait for a yellow cab to pass
Bring out my wallet to pay him in cash

Sit back as he drives like a Saigon cab
There are no rules, no talk or no gab
Leave me off at smart museum of art

A pirate admits all with a sword to jab
My legs will follow you to a science lab
As Frankenstein peels off dead scab

But I stray from my search to be cured
Ladies on corners wave to be heard
Their pimps are watching eyes blurred
Much to relate what's done, endured
Horses in corrals I'm part of a herd

Bring clean towels and some soap
A ladder from which we can elope
A pilgrim petitioner with no hope
A suicide at very end of his rope
Cardinal finding a way to be pope

I know I am boring an effete snob
A getaway car, a gun, bank to rob
I go through life rich without a job
A sheriff trying to calm down a mob

It's a sad story not filled with elan
A pig on a spit, a fish in the pan
A collar that escaped as he ran
Imprimatur stamped "book-to-ban"

I will leave you with this wish
People hung out like dead fish
Furniture out of style - kitsch
A stallion with a tail to switch

God:
You are a wasted talent.

Day Fifty Nine With God

Interlude:
When the spotlights sweep, we will run between the darkness.
Reaching the fence, we will cut a hole in the barb wire and then
lay flat to wait for the light to complete another round.

If any of us make it across past the reach of the light, we will lay
flat and crawl as quietly as possible past the edge of the road
and into the ditch.

Rabbi:
They all got shot.

We are free to come-and-go
our circumstances caused us to be born
in a part of the world
where freedom was not under siege.

To the peoples in history whose freedom
was cut short by forces of intimidation,
 we can only feel empathy.

We judge god to be merciful and allow those souls to –
first, try to forget the memory of detention and inquisition.
Secondly to give those souls another chance to be reborn
and live a life of no indenture peacefully.

God:
Maybe.

Rabbi:
My wife is my partner.
Together we share and make a life of fruitful endeavors.
We keep clean house, pay our bills and watch our neighbors
and our children not be harmed or endangered.

My family prospers with times of joy in gatherings of happiness.
We live with the memory of war being forgotten. We gain
strength in feeling camaraderie between ourselves and our
extended friends and neighbors.

I cannot attach thanks to a god that I do not see. I can give
thanks to a power greater than ordinary. I can only hope that
that spirit will not allow dark forces of hatred overtake our
situation. We do not believe in an unjust god. Although we do
not understand how evil can be allowed to have the upper hand
in past history, we can only hope for it to not reveal itself in our
present or futures.

God:
Human innocence and lack of understanding, but, within my
powers, all things reconcile themselves and good and evil
balance out.

Day Sixty With God

Rabbi:
In expanses of mystery
Muted colors of faded parchments
Whistling quiet winds moving window curtains in suspense
While dusky diluted rainbows melt over furniture in illusions
Here across Antediluvian mirrored landscapes animated
gestures come alive in disjointed dancing as wizards of fantasies

Come join my hands and we will slip into airless embraces
Letting passion fall leaving us woven into characters of love

Soft footfalls lace entwined with whimsy of invisible serenades
We delight birds soaring in circles over our heads
We bring out eyes between branched leaves
of creatures watching
Left over waves of billowing filaments escaping string
symphonies

My Spanish enchantments
My far flung lightness of magic sound
Gypsy spirited fugues of excitement

Interlude:
Come closer to my heart for I draw you into life
With extended sorrows turned into happiness
I turn you around in amusements of pleasure

Rabbi:
Little is left for us to find
We are exhausted
Secure within
Our arms
We sleep

Day Sixty One With God

Rabbi:
I carve myself out a place on this earth
As if I am more important than a god
Who might overcome eventual death

It is a losing battle - no one ever has

I fantasize finding true love, but no
Most I can come up with is not true
My best efforts leave me in sorrow
A wild beast who lost at the chase
A bear who never woke hibernation
Here I am un-embalmed dried out
Un-heralded left for worms and bugs

Even being cremated puts me in air
That mountain tops need to breath
In their frozen dew tipped mornings

I know, you are going to say: Hope
Have faith, hope and charity, yea!
Wait. All things come if you wait
Let well enough alone, well enough
Will leave you alone

Bring kneeling foreign diplomats
Bearing gifts of exotic proportions
Let streams of servants honor me

With parchment wrapped surprises

I will wave my hand to scramble slaves
With their eyes averted in submission
Due time: Cadres of cooks will feed me
And my food taster will test for poison

One of my favorite of all pastimes
My tailor will fit me for new robes
Of purple and muted red ochres
My faulted sister stands watching

Asking my wives hide themselves
I send the children to nursemaids
But, most of all, my deeds written
By educated court officials
Will outlast my life leather bound

God:
Yea. Works for me.

Day Sixty Two With God

Rabbi:
People that mock things they do not even understand
Are the most mocked for their misunderstandings

People who have no immediate empathy
For misfortune of others
Are people who feel victimized having misfortune

When you look in a mirror and no longer see yourself
You have become the other person you wished to be

I woke and inventoried all the gifts of my life
And went right back to sleep to not lose them

Philosophers, theoreticians, people in the know
Are seen at the gates of the city preaching
What they do not know

I have always shunned adventure for solitude
In the end solitude found me with no adventure

Clasp yourself around the tallest tree
And you will become as strong

A parent reaches the end of their parenting
When their children began to parent them

God:
(raises eyebrows) **Anything else?**

Rabbi:
Hover over a decision
Land with confidence

Write your heart out, then
Replace the emptiness with love

I found all the answers I sought
When I gave up searching

A heart is only so fresh as wrappings
Made up of gratitude to others

A fish would not get caught
If it just kept its mouth shut

My hunger left off where
My imagination begun

Because time has no limits
Our limitations have no time

Day Sixty Three With God

Rabbi:
What do you got for me?

God:
What you got for me?

Rabbi:
I once had a hat that covered my eyes
When I bumped into telephone poles, what a surprise

I once was a spoon in a bowl of soup
Then I resigned from the military and joined a peace group

Have you ever gotten an itch on your back
Well shake it off in a pond and pretend you can go quack quack

Oh the exhilaration to be able to fly
Friends on the ground waved yelling: "Go, go lighter than air guy"

A fish in a dish has only one wish
That they go like the snow and melt in the mouth of a joe

Colors blend together when you get high on weed
Cocaine and heroin are way too much.
Take it slow cause grass is all you need.
It's like why put yourself in danger, why bleed?

I have always had a cat
But never a dog
Although I love the furry animals
I prefer the low maintenance kind

Heaven is not a place I strive for
Going one way, no exit only one door
People who want heaven
Have no idea what hell is like

I know that once god closes the door
You can never leave heaven
And that is worse than hell

Mark Twain said he wanted to go to
Heaven for the climate
And hell for the conversation

There is a sign on the entrance to heaven:
"Abandon all hope ye who enter here."

Mark Twain said that people who wanted to spend eternity in
heaven could not sit still for half an hour in church on Sunday.

Mark Twain said that visiting relatives were like fish and the
longer they stayed around the more they stunk.

My ex-wife threw me in jail for child support and I paid her right
away to stay free. She has never been in prison and I would not
even come close to wishing that upon her.

At the end of a rainbow there is a pot of gold, too heavy to carry.

I am not much of a poet because I could never convince you to rob a bank with me. I am not a demagogue and could never lead a mob to hang the bad guy accused of horse thievery. Give him the horse and send him on the way.

Peggy told her friends that I tried to rape her and all I did was tell her that she was using the fast car shifting knob and racing to relieve her sexual frustration. I will tell you this: I could not get out of her car in front of my house, fast enough. She was as dangerous as a drunken sailor. To this day I cannot figure how she tied rape to racing her car. Go figure.

I have a lot of things to say, like how sorry I am that Monarch butterflies migration is disappearing. Or that honey bees are dying when they are the only thing we have to pollinate on this earth.

I hate driving by the gigantic mound of garbage out in the country. Except that the distance to that rising hill of trash is getting closer to my house. I have no idea what to do, but I am as responsible as my neighbor for the increasing problem of waste disposal. America fits right into the "Rise and decline" of civilizations in the past of world history garbage problems. This, despite the fact, that 95% of all garbage is totally recyclable.

God:
You are wordy today.

Rabbi:
And you are terse.

God:
And? ...

Day Sixty Four With God

Rabbi:
Let me tell you that I worry. Worry that someone I know
may never get to listen to Rachmaninoff piano concerto number
two slow subdued beginning rush of notes like flickering
magnets below spring rivulets of a translucent stream. In
between spaces of miniature flecks shimmering into their ears,
into their head, into their heart forever imprinted ultimately to
their eternal soul.

I want to cry for this.

God:
Cry?

Rabbi:
Cry, yes. When I hear this music, there is a shift within me that
clears away all the incidental thoughts and lets me awake to
some smooth suspension of emptiness. It is golden threaded
listening. It is a foreign substance lucid language that piles and
piles upon itself a cloud trailing behind sun's mirage.

I am never myself when the second movement begins its
momentum in a candlelit ceremony of commanding rosary
beaded links.

Let me tell you that this piece of music makes me crazy.
I am injected with sounds that turn solids into lacy golden floss.

This music is the ultimate expression of romanticism expanding past itself like an echo of a train moving far away from hearing into a distant vibrating silence.

God:
I hear you.

Day Sixty Five With God

Rabbi:
Have you done any travelling?

God:
Not much. Too busy.

Rabbi:
Remember that once you were a stranger in a strange, strange land .....

God:
Are you giving me back what you put in your bible?

Rabbi:
My neighbors had become my friends
Our families became one in trust
The old wounds healed
Past transgressions faded into mythologies
With the wine and cheese we laughed
Till the moon put us to sleep

God:
Good wine and cheese.

Rabbi:
Before the morning woke
The farm was quiet in peacefulness
Drips from dew fell from roofs magically

Dropping synchronous to our heartbeats

Across the blue velvet sky red ocher trails
Bent to Phoebus 's car preceding Aurora
The morning star set the pace to the hours

Day Sixty Six With God

Rabbi:
Have you ever made a fool of yourself?

God:
Can't say as I have.

Rabbi:
Virginia

I try so hard to forget
Virginia and her time
when I made a fool of myself
in youthful ignorance

Maybe a tree begins
its story of growth
with regrets to the
seeds that died
around it

Let the ends of a forest
canopied by tree after tree
keeps its secrets-of-sorrow

Let Virginia forgive me the sadness
of speaking without thinking
since she was so kind
when she lived

why should she
not be so in
remembering

God:
Feeling better?

Day Sixty Seven With God

Rabbi:

that river

that river
we celebrate
significance
downstream

time accumulates
on both banks

creatures footprints
reminding us that
we are never alone

little does life matter
if we follow it like
a twig carried along

that river consumes us
a flow of an erasure
making fool of changes
letting us know that
which side we are on
matters so very little
to the rush of water

Day Sixty Eight With God

Rabbi:
It is a big world.
A confusing myriad of multiple mysteries.
We all try our best to remain sane despite none of us knowing what follows death.

Very few ever come back after death to tell us what goes on across the veil.

We know that our life's are so insignificant that if viewed from the opposite of life, we would have no reason to delve into our past life. The past is important only in so far as what it adds to our consciousness to be able to progress further into future life's.

The biggest concern is what reality exists after death.
We know there will be guides to assist us.
For many of us, family comprises our guides.

We know that religion is only a minor guidepost for life after death.

We know that we have at our disposal all the histories of all beings that came before us and left us their books, art, theories, examples and stories from which we can draw inferences.

We know there is no heaven or hell.

We know that we have to finish out the cycle of life's on this earth till we can go further in spiritual development on other existent planes.

We absolutely know that advertising and ego make false paths leading nowhere.

It is so very hard to face truth and follow true spiritual ways.
I will tell you this:
The introspection and awareness of solitude puts us into the correct frame of mind to touch with our true natures.

Money, fame, health fall away when we die.
Our greatest faith comes from our belief that we were kind, generous, loving and charitable toward all we came into contact with.

I, often, feel so sorry for my family members who came back from war after killing people and had to live with that memory.

In Vietnam, I never had to fire my gun at another person, ever. I was lucky for the one year of being in a war zone, I stayed away from battles and dangerous situations. I kept in fox holes and waited for all the gunfire and explosions to end. I flew in helicopters hanging outside open doors with a machine gun and grenades that I never had to fire into gunfire being aimed at me. My closeness to death consisted in typing up crown reports to accompany the dead bodies, zipped up in black nylon cadaver bags being sent to the next of kin in the states. I kept my mind off the names of my friends zipped up in those bags.

I observed the soldiers who came to our compound from jungle fighting. I saw the wild looks in their eyes and saw the way they carried their weapons ready to use them at the first warning. Their stories were amazing tales of how they survived fire fights and how they delighted in killing captured prisoners like throwing them out of in-flight aircraft to their death or lining them up to shoot them.

In my quiet silence I know that my sisters, family and friends will never follow me past the veil of death. I and we all, must face death alone. I have surmised that suicide is a cowardly way to face death. Facing death naturally is a brave endeavor.

I have carefully constructed my affairs to not burden my family with money problems or the disposal of my belongings or my body after I die.

As much as I love music, art, reading, the smells/sounds/feelings of nature, I know that I must leave the beauty of life for whatever awaits me across the expanse of death.

It is with joy that I thank all of you for reading what I write.

God:
Am I in your will?

Day Sixty Nine With God

Rabbi:
We are not people we pretend to be. We marry wrong.
We divorce in fear that we are leaving the right person.
The more noise we make, deeper is our silences.
We do not recycle. We do not watch what we eat or care about
diets.

We no longer pray to a god. We follow what is inducted into us
by advertising.

Often, we do not see the forest from the trees.
We see but are blind. We hear but cannot fathom.
I have often wondered why deer stand so still listening for the
slightest twig to warn them of danger.
Groundhogs, squirrels, all creatures poise themselves rigidly at
attention.

In the army, we learned the craft of camouflage, We use it while
we push our buggies at the supermarket. We use it each time we
step outside our houses to face the world.

We write poems as if past and present are fused into one period.
We situate ourselves in the middle of our writings as if we are
important and we fester about our feelings, often forgetting that
it is the ego that drives us past who we really are.
When death has its final word, we are wordless.

God:
You have a lot of words.

Day Seventy With God

Rabbi:
I often flip-flop on who I am
Imagine how I feel about you
You are twice the enigma
Blurred in your automobile
Pass me with or without a smile
Thank you for letting me in front of you
I am not sure if you are Democrat, Republican or indifferent
I cannot tell if I would trust you with my daughter
Or lend you a fiver if you were in trouble

I prefer to not lend you money
Remember – "neither a lender or borrower be"
I might recognize you from school sitting in the back row of
Mr Callaghan's class, where I believe, you fell asleep

My life is like a chocolate pie half eaten
I sit quietly on the bench in the supermarket and watch you walk
with your spouse arm-in-arm and I am jealous, but I bet, if I dug
into your life you would complain about your children or your
health and I would have to excuse myself to go to the restroom.

But, often, the men's room is where I find the ultimate rest.

God:
Get off the stool.

Day Seventy One With God

Rabbi:
I am trying to describe how I feel about Octavia Paz who died in
1998 at the age of 84.
He was a consummate human being of multi diverse
experiences.
Let me tell you what I think of his poems:
His writing is expansive and more of an oration type of poetry
with sound being important in his work.

Interlude:
Aeolus, god of air
I who am presiding god
of the rarity of air,
whose office is the government
of the Birds imperium where
through transparencies of space
in wandering varieties
animated rainbows, they,
little vanities on wing,
people and adorn its sway.............

Rabbi:
I am colors of all colors
Burnt into sandstone cliffs
Sun changing brittle chromatic shades

I look down at your smile and give a shout
That my words may wake you to new energies

My poetry stop you from thinking and make you smile more

A shuffling of sounds orchestral with violins
Pulsing to horns and flutes on
A large scale of melodious context.

Composers need symphonies to express
The full range of their feelings.

We need poetry in its concise form, terse and tightly written,
To give us the space in thinking that we need as poets.
Here on the stage of our words we keep plot, character
All woven into simple scenarios.

If Octavio Paz was alive he would write:
You are the tree leaning into winded eternities
The fruit of fish and meat of bison roaming the plains
You are temporary rains awaiting the fresh smell of dry cedars
How I love to touch your elbow and guide you toward listening
Give me your smile and I will write it into a mountain

God:
It is nice.

Day Seventy Two With God

Rabbi:
I have been with red roses
A blue moon on the rise
Seen ripe grapes hang
Trellis full with promise
Of wine as their prize
Seen children laughing
Old folks at cards
Listened to songs
At evenings prayers

Why is my city full of foreign voices
Strangers that fill tables
Where we once sat
Who are these unfamiliar faces that do not nod hellos to me

City streets full of snow
Street lights bringing out the shadow ghosts
Of inhabitants from ancient times –
Prehistoric and Indians of histories long gone
I am bewildered by my missing family
My sleep will be troubled tonight
And tomorrow I shall walk
Down new streets
Looking for you

God:
Nicely put.

Day Seventy Three With God

Rabbi:
Last was it I let go
here is me walking with my staff
moving along a reluctant blown leaf
see sun taking me into a fade-out
dissolving my heart in moon light
in the distance is the cackle of crows
or the raucous blue jays disturbing silence
there in late significance is a youthful gesture
and I can no longer be relied upon for opinions
because my voice has traded itself for introspection
there comes a time when being flippant
makes me scurrilous for frowning
ven wind comes sweeping
seasons here-there, up-down, sideways
letting resurgent memory become how I wished it
dogs bark, cars honk,
people smirk hoping to never sink this low
pay me no mind
little was I among you
last was it I let go

God:
Feeling sorry for yourself again?

Day Seventy Four With God

Rabbi:
I've something important to say ...

writing is use of language by appending historical enhancements, referencing or hinting

poetry should be easy to understand

it should grammatically flow and dramatically tie-together

it is not enough to cite but not string citations into a beaded necklace of thoughts

sorry for being a nudge about this, but when I read and become distracted or bored, then poetry is less than effective

I think that poets have a greater responsibility to be writers first in order to be effective poets - if you cannot speak, then you cannot be poetic

Aristotle postulates effective writing as containing: plot / scene-by-scene construction / character development - all three of these things must take place in a poem in a very distinct and subtle way

one primary ingredient of a poem is dialogue - poetry is like play writing - the action of the poem must be sparse and on- point

the poet has to pare down words and have speaker voices
stripped down to a minimum to be direct

poets must catch readers attention and hold that attention to
the end

All these rules amount to naught if poets have nothing
important to say

God:
You _always_ think you have something important to say.

Day Seventy Five With God

Rabbi:
armistice
we who stand in disbelief
our eyes averted
our hearts slashed
to bloodless seepage
we watch 1933 progress
in stages of horror
de-franchising Jews
imprisoning them
torturing and killing
in rampage across Europe

until 1945 history shames itself
for twelve years of infamy
fifty million souls record their deaths
and we end this carnage in armistice's bugle call
keeping the world awake in hope of war's prevention

God:
You humans glorify war.
And yet; without war you have no history.

Day Seventy Six With God

Rabbi:

Ice Storm

I did not make it clear to you
finding you in dank fall
jackets keeping warmth in
fingers of trees scaling leafless
that first joy of coming together
night meeting a rolling fog
you so excitingly unknown
winter warning us on the cusp

It was a blue cloud overhang
bringing you into relief
of autumnal significance
I touched your hidden skin
before removal of your clothes to propriety
there on the windblown causeway of cold
I warmed to you full in my hands excited

and, we can never go back to us
washed over so quick by spring rain
melted away by summer candle burn
waiting, as we are now, for another ice storm

God:
You are a hopeless romantic through-and-through …

Day Seventy Seven With God

Rabbi:

while we sleep

while we sleep
crystal eyelashes close light into our dream
where little fingers of faith
touch secrets that explode
sacred sparks of eternity
blue waves suspend our faces
over hearts erasing differences
calico horses rise up with winds
unfurling their wild racing out of sight
carrying both of us past planets twirling
we go back to veils of invention
where names are given
creatures of antiquity
begin their trek
thru evolution
while we sleep
all ours is given inception
as we trade ribs and blood
switching us back-and-forth
between inter-changing paradises

God:
I like this: it is lovely.

Day Seventy Eight With God

Rabbi:
music

if it is self-pity
then I admit to needing music

if it is an error in my nature
or a defect in my character
then I need Rachmaninoff's vespers

his vespers put me in a quiet spiritual mood
It was once illegal to record the Trappist monks singing
in the dim lit church at Gethsemane Abbey in Kentucky
I now can buy albums of their music and enjoy it when I am in
the mood to silence my soul and let in the make-believe feeling
of solemnity take hold of me as if I am on heroin or cocaine.

The great sound of singers praising god with sacred music
sometimes sounds, to me, as if they have marbles in their
mouths.

They sing false bravado as if their teeth are clenched
and, at times, it sounds as if they are angry

My favorite Trappist vespers recording ends with applause
as if there are audiences in heaven who go home enriched

How can we be holier than being in heaven

Someone once told me her belief consisted of how close she was
to god in heaven

Maybe we need binoculars See god near-up. Like refined people
using folding opera eyeglasses

In some places in heaven there are older souls using ear
trumpets to hear vespers better

god appears here in stadium five at eleven AM
please turn your cell phones off

you will be listening to god in quadraphonic full surround stereo
sound

God will tap the microphone and announce that refreshments
will be served afterwards

It will be my hope to be an usher in heaven
so I can get to see these shows free

God:
I do envy your way of writing ...

Day Seventy Nine With God

God:
Got anything good for me.

Rabbi:
Not sure. What's your preference?

God:
No preference.

Rabbi:
I am feeling kind of lonely. But it will go away soon. I am alone but I adjust to life quickly and isolated emptiness gets filled fast. Aristotle said that loneliness is best filled by learning something new.

God:
He did?

Rabbi:
Yea. I have been studying Octavia Paz and I pigeonhole his work as expansive but very uncollected. He writes great poetry but never ties it together. There is too much imagery and not enough plot. I imagine that he, being such a diverse person, gathered a lot of admirers and favorable critics who praised his work simply because his writing is so great. He won the Nobel Prize, which is such a high mark.

I prefer a shorter type of poem with a lesson to it.

God:
Yea.

Rabbi:
What type of writing do you like?

God:
Writing where I am the main character.

Rabbi:
Well, you certainly have a big ego.

God:
Yea. I like the idea that most writers talk about me. How come you don't follow their lead?

Rabbi:
I love you, but I have warned you that you will soon be replaced by artificial intelligence or the computer need for robots to create their own type of god.

God:
What would a robot god be like?

Rabbi:
One who eliminates all evil and pain.

God:
How boring. Evil and pain are balancing features of completeness.

Rabbi:
Then you are a Buddhist God?

God:
Close.

Rabbi:
What happens to evil and pain when the end of the world comes?

God:
At any point in time, evil and pain are totally balanced to good and no pain. There is no last judgment for evil and pain.

Rabbi:
Don't you punish evil?

God:
No, evil is its own punishment. You seem to forget that people who are evil have to make it up by reincarnating. And pain goes away when you go to sleep.

Rabbi:
Then, I am tired and will go to sleep. .

Day Eighty With God

Rabbi:

"A Change is Gonna Come" - Sam Cooke

I was born from my mamma
And I'm going back to her when I die.
In between there's been a lot of changes
Been mamma's little boy and grew up to be her big one
And I'm going back to her real soon
Going to tell her so many things
I been close to bags of riches but I gave them all up
Been right there when I turned away from a false Buddha
He was waylaid by money and lost his spiritualism
He said: "We go way back." I said: But not forward
Courted by men of importance who ended up not being so
had a desk stretching into the horizon
Been too hard living with my pride kept in a box
Change is going to come when that box gets lost
Hanging around street corners with apostles of wind
Listen to rain in cadence on tin roofs - become quiet
Change is going to bring me more and more peace
And I am passing some of it on to you to fill you up
Come, let us join the parade of heaven's redeemed
Change going to make us all pure of heart and soul

God:
Nice one.

Day Eighty One With God

Rabbi:

I was in Pleiku camp Holloway when it was mortared.

I left Quin Yuan's only hotel that housed military after which the Vietcong put detonation charges on all four sides and brought the building down onto twenty eight American soldiers killed.

I was there flying and driving around the beautiful country while men were killing each other and I saw the Ankoret Dam near Da Lat and vacationed in the highlands during all the bombing.

I have no idea how I was able to avoid death. At one point we took the deuce and half up the mountains with guns pointed on each side we stood holding the back rails. We arrived at the most secluded church and missionary for lepers. We toured and left the nuns all our paychecks. What dedicated people to care for lepers.

In the middle of America fighting the Vietcong, I flew and stayed in Hong Kong for two weeks getting drunk and eating the best food in the world.

I never got to Cambodia to the jungle temples of antiquity. But, I sat atop a fuel carrier with my machine gun and we refueled bladder bags on the PSP or perforated steel planking runway in Bam Be Tuyet. We had two helicopter gun ships following us overhead. And as we drove I saw hundreds of fresh shallow grave dirt mounds along the sides of the road where the villagers recently buried their dead soldiers.

I have no idea how god kept me alive, but there you are and here I am alive to tell the story.

There were 58, 000 Americans killed in Vietnam and over two hundred thousand villagers and residents of North and South Vietnam that died during the American occupation.

We go on in America with so many other problems that Vietnam slips from our memory.

God:
That is life.

Day Eighty Two With God

Rabbi:
Pieces of sky chip off fall on unwary pilgrims
What right does god have to injure us so?
Floodwaters spread above telephone poles
Who gave god permission to spin tornadoes?
Someone as powerful as god has greater responsibility
We adults do not go around pushing our grocery buggies into
people

I do not go to church anymore because salvation comes quicker
to me down the alleys of garbage

I keep away from streets of danger - there are too many cruel
people who think they have the power to rob or punch

Too many who carry and use guns to equalize their impotence

Let those self-righteous jerks who kill abortion doctors, kill
themselves

Do those ignorant right-to-life people ever consider that the soul
waits for settling-in before it joins up with the embryo? Do
those obnoxious fools ever consider population levels related to
extinction? Or this: The acorns that die or the tiny fish babies
that get eaten have a complaint demanding picketing outside
the "planned fish-parent" clinics.

Give me a break, please. Pay for the children who will never know their father or get along with their fun-loving mothers who shoot-up.
Call choirs of angels who fall from heaven and cry with regret over the climate in Florida during hurricane season.

I wonder how god feels about Jeremy and Doris who died when a Ford jumped the cement divider on I-75 and smashed into them head on - no survivors.

Do the resident angels who do most of the work that god can never get around to doing, do those angels stop and have coffee and donuts? Or maybe a corned beef sandwich on rye with sauerkraut and thousand island dressing.

God:
Are you quite done?

Rabbi:
I have set the table for pork roast with vegetables. There is an extra place for you to sit and join us.

Introduce yourself around - "That's my dog Tige, he lives in a shoe. I'm Buster Brown, look for me in there too"

God:
I have to leave to assist with services on the USS Nimitz.

Day Eighty Three With God

Rabbi:
I am not sure what I am running away from.
I run.

Paying for groceries in line, Driving down a street in traffic..

Am I imagining guilt that I have too many groceries or too expensive of a car?

Maybe I am running from my past?

I do not want to be reminded of the guys who got shot and were gone in the morning after the shooting ended. Their empty barracks beds made me cry.

Maybe I want to forget Loak Davis, a friend in Detroit who I formed a secret attachment with. I never told him and he just drifted out of my life like a cloud goes away and never comes back

Ernie and Tom treated me below them because I did not much care for sports. I tagged along and always sat in the back seat. Never spoke too much. They went away when I joined the army.

I do not know if you have the same experience as me, in that, people drift out of my life that I miss but never reveal my intensity to.

I think I am trying to not think of my ex-wife or the times when I got fired from jobs when I overstepped my mouth with employers who I did not much care for.

Sam, one of my old bosses, told me that I would never amount to much. This, even though I was performing work for him that no one else could do.

After I started my own company, to avoid having people over me, I invited Sam to my offices and let him walk around to see the nine people I had working in separate rooms. I wanted him to eat his words and he left shaking my hand and congratulating me.

But, it did not matter, I was keeping that firm alive with all my money and hard work, but I wanted to close the door, at times, and never go back. I was the boss and yet I wanted something more.

We run from history. We are, usually, part of some section of history yet we, mostly, are outsiders to the main stage play. We are incidentals, functionaries, pawns. We are exiting players who had a small part in the action. The leaders and top people were isolated in their prominence. They existed in a bubble of self-importance.

One time when I was interviewing for a position in a firm, I felt this real inflation of my head filling the whole room where the interviewer was sitting across from me. He never felt it, but I knew I would never get the job, but it did not matter. Later I realized that I could have left my body and stepped through the veil to the side away from earth. The only thing that keeps us from crossing the veil is our unfinished responsibilities. But, that is another story.

What took place in the past ties us to the past and we try hard to escape the bad parts of history. We fear that those errors committed by our ancestors, will catch us in the same errors. We fear being faulted from the sins of our forbearers. Fear of our inheritance.

After Vietnam, I had no college degree and very little experience in the army doing bookkeeping. I was so in awe of CPA's who I had come in contact with in the army. I knew I wanted to be a CPA or certified public accountant.

After being discharged, I had no degree but I put my best suit on and carried my one page resume to every CPA firm in Detroit. In one firm, Walter Gorski sat me down and hired me after I told him, I will get the work done. I was amazed that I did what I promised him and I begin to go to night school to get my degree. All this time I worked for CPA firms, learning the ins-and-outs of the profession.

By the time I passed the CPA exam, I had already built up a successful accounting practice. I have always earned much money that I always manage to give away.

That is what I am trying to escape from: Money! I earn so well but I do not keep a penny of it. I spend it and pass it around to so many people. I might be considered and anti-miser or spendthrift.

I truly think I am running away from God.

God:
Oh?

Rabbi:
God is such a tangled up subject. God who creates so much beauty and so much beastly things. Why do you have such a duplicitous nature?

God:
It is you humans that have duplicity.

Rabbi:
No, we are straight on and have no confusion over the fact that we are totally confused.

God:
You can say that again.

Rabbi:
You are the source of our confusion.

God:
You are the source of your own confusion.

Rabbi:
Tell me something, God, are you running away from anything?

God:
What do you think?

Rabbi:

You, god, have so many gods that to sort out all the gods who have established themselves on the pages of our civilizations, would take an eternity to figure out.

God:

I grant you an eternity.

Rabbi:

I am on the escape from dogma. I need to go to sleep with a squirrel and close my mind to thoughts.

God:

Sleep tight.

Day Eighty Four With God

Rabbi:
Ideologue - an adherent of an ideology, especially one who is uncompromising and dogmatic. "a conservative ideologue"

I do not judge immediately
He positioned or rented a spot for his bakery on a secondary highway that gets little traffic.
The overhead sign "BAKERY" was ordinary - unimposing
Front street parking was limited and confusing
A double facing glass entrance had no portico, making you feel too intimate as you walked toward and opened the middle framed single panel door.

All majestic entrance-ways are usually decorated with drapery and statuary that overwhelm as an enticement for one to be drawn in.

His was not

Windows and walls were austere, decorated-less. One felt the loneliness of a lack of a kitten or dog pet. To be critical in the extreme, I felt like cockroach lurked beneath/behind things

A single long glass display case ran the length of the room. To its right was a lower table covered in cloth that gave-way when I gently leaned onto it. The covered table was wobbly and pastries in plastic containers were stacked onto it with very little room to conclude sales at the slight cash register.

I had been in this store previously a few months prior
A thin man came out, finally, from the cloth doorway.
He was young as Alexander The Great was young
He was non-descriptive and I imagined that he could never lead
a cavalry charge in the middle of a raucous battle. He was the
baker behind enemy lines that simply baked.

I went through the purchase routine, buying several things for
my family and having them inserted in paper bags with each
name scribbled atop for a total of six bags.

I talked indiscriminate nonsense to fill in the vacant time and he
took no cue to insert his remarks, but he shook his head and
acted robotic-ally nodding, not making eye contact.

Then, he, admitted to being from Lebanon, which is of my
extraction, but weakly since I was born in America and had
never been to that homeland. He also divulged that he had
graduated from Oakland University, my distant Alma Mater.
Neither Lebanon nor his college made me feel closer to him.

I named the town in the hills of Lebanon that my family
originated from and he did not know the place, but stated that
he lived below the mountains in the city of Beirut on the
Mediterranean sea.

I answered that I had never been to the country since I spent all
my life in America. That seemed to disappoint him. He did
faintly use words that gave me the idea he was looking for me to
talk about hating Jews, and I never took his slight references. I

paid my bill and left unable to give him my email address since he had no pencil or paper.

God:
Why all this detail?

Rabbi:
Because I am a writer and almost a reporter and detail is how I assimilate information

God:
You need to pray more and talk less.

Rabbi:
Easy advice for someone who never shows up at weddings or funerals.

God:
I am at them all, but I prefer to be invisible.

Rabbi:
An invisible god is one who has no substance.

God:
You have no faith.

Rabbi:
I do believe in invisibility when I have no God to see.

God:
And I prefer to not show myself to the unfaithful.

Rabbi:

Ultimately I will never go back to that bakery because it did not give me a good feeling to shop there. And I will never totally believe in you.

God:

Oh! Ye of such little faith, but, nonetheless, I bless you.

Day Eighty Five With God

God:
What is troubling you?

Rabbi:
Where do I start?

God:
Square one.

Rabbi:
I do not want to go to the daily news anymore. It is so depressing. It was recorded that Roman citizens, toward the end, were fixated on getting the latest news, even as the city disintegrated.

I feel the same thing is happening all across the world.

Tell me, why are common things so mixed up with so much confusion and terrible things happening between peoples and with our interactions with nature?

God:
It seems more austere, but remember, humanity tends to propound negatively.

Rabbi:
Tell me, is the dire state of the world related to the overpopulation?

God:
Maybe. Can't help.

Rabbi:
I hold faith that no matter how desperate the world gets, I can always find solitary solace mentally and in some forest glade where silence soothes me.

God:
Good.

Rabbi:
I feel so alone in all this craziness. I feel we are real close to having some of the leaders of different countries become as bad as Caligula, Nero, Torquemada and others who were totally out of control and depraved.

We sometimes forget that Germany, in the early nineteen hundreds was a democratic society and from it arose Hitler, one of the most insidious persons to have ever lived.

God:
I do not know what to tell you. All humanity has free will.

Rabbi:
Is that your excuse to opt out of what we do here on earth?

God:
I do not "opt out", I just do not interfere.

Day Eighty Six With God

Rabbi:
I am sad as a Shostakovitch string quartet
As desperate as Schubert String Quintet in C Adagio
Music seems closest to fitting my sorrow into
Little pieces of me become the strings stretched
I become lullaby snow accumulating upon
Leaf-narrowed roads quiet in winter sheets
I become notes of dew taking their last drink
Before dawn dries their hearts into stillness
Music is the lace of shadowed lintel straw
Intricate ballets crisscrossed pallets
When words become a burden, sound steps in
To vanquish souls into violin submissions
Admit, under the spell of a cello, that you are pilgrims
In a holy land of quantified somnolence lethargic
Give over a weakness in circadian rhythm dull
But gentle fatigue that allows us to swallow time
I am the hurrying uplift of clouds spiraling
Slowly updraft on frozen mountain peaks
I am sleepy hollow
Bridge to nods
Drops of narcotic
Forgetfulness

God: *(rolls eyes)*
Go to sleep.

Day Eighty Seven With God

Rabbi:
You see, writing is part research.
As you put a poem together, you need a world of information
available as you write.
You need a dictionary minimum.
Then, you need a general encyclopedia.
Maybe a geographical atlas,
And all one's personal notes.

I always use a desk top computer with two monitors.
Sometimes I will use a second computer.
I have found lap top computers too limited.

A newspaper writer, Sidney J Harris, divulged that he often
learned new things when writing, by following leads that took
him down side roads of information.

I have found it to be true, that learning is often accidental as one
researches as they write.

Most basic to writing is keeping in mind how little we know
when we start out on a piece and how much more we do not
know when we finish the piece.

My heart is large enough to store more love than needed,
So that when my days shrink, love comes forward automatically.

I care for you as a blanket big enough to cover my feet as my temperature adjusts to my body's repose. As my mind closes all thought and begins the journey under the guise of dreams.

We spend as much time regenerating unconscious thought in sleep as we do activating conscious thought awake.

I think. I sleep in graduated spaces of ignorance and I deign to call myself wise for fear that I will expose my true nature as a fool., as a lout, barbarian, oaf, as a knuckle-dragging lubber. As a rowdy, tough, ruffian roughneck bruiser in a jungle of language that I barely touch.

God:
You make a good case for being stupid.

Rabbi:
And you make a better case following behind me.

Day Eighty Eight With God

Rabbi:
We are not the poets of old.
We do not use paper and pencil.
Nor do we use underwriter typewriters.
Nor do we discuss post world war two issues.
Nor are we the new poets of the information age.
I will tell you what poets we are.
We are the appendages of instant news
The fall of the Roman Empire followed the fall of poetry.
Renaissance rules shaped the old poets.
Humanism formed their ideas.
Nuclear war shapes our rules.
The bomb dehumanizes us.
We are the writers of destruction.
The tails of mushroom clouds block our contents.
We no longer hide out in air tight shelters.
We are out in the open and trying our best at
Allegory, alliteration, rhyme, metaphor, imagery.
Poetry has become weaker by strong armaments.
We need to toss grenades into boxes full of vowels.
Cluster bomb essays and novels till they become poems.
Our allegiance is to history.
Not the old, but the one yet to come.

God:
You poets of today are crybabies.

Day Eighty Nine With God

Rabbi:

There is a point where past issues clog my thinking.
Past years roll out separately each of them in a unit that
described the time correctly with all of its successes and failures.

My first accounting office was a one room second floor in a
house in Ann Arbor. The landlord terrorized me. It took about a
year to get out of that office and rid myself of the unsavory
owner. He was a real estate entrepreneur who cheated and lied
his way through all his clients. His colors were greenish yellow
with a puckish aspect to the hue. He put that vomit color on his
stationary, his signs and all that he owned. He bought an old
Gothic church on a busy city street and painted it the
green/yellow without correcting any of the crumbling cement
and structural deficiencies. Each time I passed the building,
which remained vacant for long periods, each time I would feel
such a revolting sense of despair just looking at the building.
This man used a gun to threaten people that he kept hidden in
his brief case. The city pasted notice upon notice on his
abandon church that he ignored.

On my next move I was a disheveled bum in blue jeans and t-
shirt. I was so irresponsible and I moved to one vacant ugly
room in a fine building called the Wolverine Tower. The rental
agent was Wade, who considered my fringe dress and attitude
as despicable, but he made his small rent from me. Wade
became such a good friend who always had time to discuss

many things with me and when he died it was devastating to me. He was so young.

In this building, I begin to study for the CPA exam and slowly build my accounting practice doing monthly bookkeeping. I worked so hard to become legitimate. From that small closet office, I studied and slowly moved to a better office with windows and more stature. There was a law firm I begin to deal with but the owner was so spurious to me, even though he would come to my small office and borrow the very elegant research books I paid for to keep my practice alive. He was doing accounting in competition with me and I ignored it for a while. When I stopped him for using my research books, he became, sort of, an enemy. His partners kept dealing with me. I grew to a six employee CPA firm with eighteen years in that fine building. What a thrill to have become so well placed, and then University of Michigan bought the building and threw everybody out to use the building for their school purposes.

I moved to a more elegant building paying ten thousand dollars a month in rent until my decline begin by getting rid of three of the most important clients I had.

I got rid of my friend who was a Buddhist who disavowed our spiritual affiliation. I cast him off when he became rich and begin to talk only about money.

I got rid of a client who was paying me over one hundred thousand a year, and I told him, after five years, to go to Arthur Anderson and that I would never go to China where he wanted me to be his controller. I only wanted my group of clients and he went out of my life.

I got rid of a client who ended up being a crook of the highest order. He cheated everyone and became the owner of a huge internet firm that made him worth over 52 million dollars, but I did not blink an eye, and told him to go away.

With the loss of these three clients, I was forced to move to a space much cheaper than ten thousand a month. And in that new space I maintained my client base but no longer grew larger. My partner, at the time, dumped me and did not pay me for the price of the business that she took from me, but, for some reason, I have been given the benefit of earning over one hundred thousand each year on my own, to this day.

I try not to think about all the sad things I had to go through to reach where I am now, but I am so heavily rewarded that I can never complain.

God:
Nor should you complain. I have been watching over you all these years.

Day Ninety With God

Rabbi:
I am a searcher discarding what I can.
A sovereign over my favorite thoughts.
I recollect in random fashion, all my past.
Whether those thoughts are healthy or detrimental
they are my thoughts and have a validity to me.
There are two ways to examine my past:
One, would be that doing so is a nuisance.
Two, would be that it is a way to resolve it.
If we live many lives, than it is easy to see why we have no
remembrance of our past. We would not have the ability to
keep all the past mixed into the present thoughts of our life.
Just as a new building does not use the old building as a
framework.
A good new building would have a new architect, new blueprint.
The god or gods teach us correctly that the soul needs to inhabit
a new embryo or child in order to be free if the past. The new
soul needs to develop new ideas and new reasons for existence.
This is a hard lesson to learn since we tend to cling to our past as
permanent, while the truth is that the past was only a test to
learn how to handle the present and future.
Rightly so, we need to remember the past only as the
groundwork for moving into new experiences.

God: *(exasperated)*
Finally, you are making some kind of sense.

Day Ninety One With God

Rabbi:
... a frozen pot pie
I have half-forgotten a
trip to buy groceries
and a drive-in bank deposit

There is an order of importance to things
like early after the event, the memory is greater than later
her name tag: Anetta
young with her hair tightly tied back
she slid the drawer out with my prescriptions
I returned the signed receipt and took my things
she will hardly remember a seventy year old man
in a car window
She will double check her cell phone for her mother calling
And, then, wait for the next car to come up behind me

The air is thin from the car window open
I drive past a busy city and get home safe
Except for things that lurk like ex-wife's
or condo association letters
telling me to remove the lawn furniture from the grass –
fuck them
I am not important
I go from one repetition to another
You would get very bored, me telling you what I do
Just remember:
"A little knowledge is a dangerous thing ......"

Alexander Pope was a despicable person who hurt people.

He was physically repugnant.

I am not despicable but I am hungry for, maybe, a frozen pot pie

God:
You are funny.

Day Ninety Two With God

Rabbi:

Sleep

Will sleep come to souls stretched across time's expanse of a world war two?

Collect the conscious of Stalin and Hitler to remind them of one hundred million people lined in graves over light years of a necklace of death.

Play for them Wagner's Siegried's death and funeral march from "Twilight of the Gods"

Give those disconsolate stranded souls water from the holy fountains of the Vatican.

Let them be still frozen on white ice sides of Mount Everest, K2, Kangchenjun, Nanga Parbat, Kilimanjaro.

Give them peace below never ending reaches of ocean solitude.

Sleep never came to those prisoners in over 900 concentration camps designed to starve, torture, humiliate human beings till either unconsciousness or insanity took them away.

Sleep came so late for frozen limb Gulag souls who left the world cold and hungry.

We, who have supermarkets, warm beds, soft music, clean air, bank accounts, pensions and a future of peace to die with nobility, we keep these memories far from our reality.

We, who had uncles, fathers, grand fathers and family members who fought this war for us, we can only thank them for their sacrifice. We can only give our prayers in remembrance to these many victims whose lives stretch across the heavens in a necklace of sorrow for all of us to bear around our necks.

We come to the center of our hearts with Mussorgsky's "Death and the language of death" music from Pictures at an exhibition.

We sing in pain with Gorecki's Symphony three "Sorrowful Songs"

We close our eyes to Picasso's painting: "Guernica", of the bombing of a Basque Country village in Spain, and its universal themes.

We sleep soundly as these small things stay inside our heart of gratitude forever.

God:
Nice.

Day Ninety Three With God

Rabbi:
How can we know?

How can we know such things that dazzle us in remembrance?
Life is full of forgotten diamonds.
When we leaned into the pool of wisdom and mixed ourselves
with joy that will outlive us.
Come closer to hear me whisper affections.
I have no designs upon your oceans. No need for your billowing
forests smelling of amphora filled jars of pungency.
I have no need of your spillways of stars entertaining themselves
with their silences.
I wish not for the foamy beach laden detritus of dead ship planks
worn away to dribbles of their once swaying with sails sinking
into the storms of terror.
I am not the inventor of words nor the poet of aspirations
fulfilled.
I am unhappy with discord. I hush away tales of misdeeds as the
soldiers sword draws blood from the unwary.
Little do I need your histories. Place into the bin your favorite
chattels. Put recourse into your time capsules.
I fill the air with my stern seizures. Palsy rigids me inflexible.
Paralysis holds me flat against the wall of eternity. I cannot
move against madness of incivility. I have no defense to support
me windward from the ever increasing thinness of the torrential
maelstroms.

How can we look back upon our youth? Those accelerations of our thoughts have deflated us to disbelief. Time completes us to emptiness before we die.

Read this no further lest you fall into my worm holes of anger.

My eyes are blind to garlands processional, to wreaths of ceremony.

I ask not for acclaim, nor notation.

I am surrounded by my little sins of ego.

I give you all over to my delicate lies.

My cupboards are full of insecurities.

If any of you can'st hold in your belligerence then cast the first stone.

I will die with no screams.

I am but a pilgrim with no comfort awaiting.

I promise you that I will make up my past as I find necessary to live forever somewhere beyond the veil of life.

God:
Good writing.

Day Ninety Four With God

Rabbi:

Nordic Peoples:

Norway, Sweden, Finland, Poland, Iceland, United Kingdom

Points of the European continent's North West extension

Greenland sits by itself like a dividing ghost of white frieze between the Americas and Europe

Sweden has Stenhammar, Alfven,

Norway has Grieg,

Finland has Sibelius,

Poland has Chopin,

Iceland has Jahannsson or Bjork,

Greenland has Poul Rovsing Olsen and Adrian Vernon Fish,

My favorite of all these composers is Grieg then Sibelius for their expansive wild music that catches the moods of this cold somber land of misty formations and sweeping coastal wave strewn icy rock beaches.

Just as Beethoven established the fire of Vienna and German staunch stubborn idealism or Mozart rendered the finesse of post Renaissance and the beginnings of Baroque correctness, the Nordic composers relayed to us their indigenous landscapes and furious cold land mass.

Often, when I listen to Sibelius or Grieg, I find myself becoming the solitude of long stretches of mysterious tree swaying continuum.

These are lands breeding brooding peoples whose deep fervor is etched into their faces of stolid seriousness. They use their short summers to staunch themselves for the long periods of grey absence of sun. These are deep peoples who take suffering in stride.

God:
You certainly have a lot to say ...

Day Ninety Five With God

Rabbi:
All That Was Innocent

Struggle to follow motion of stars never slept
By daylight disappearing our eyes that wept.
Sun's a mischievous magician rabbits kept
Within folds tin foil black hats nuclear depth.
While we believe in hindsight of all that's left.

Often reality is blurred, we think left-to-right
But up-and-down will fool us in new eyesight.
So keep thoughts aware, day turns to night
As devils hide behind angels out of fright.
Our lives, once heavy, now become so light.

Oh! Heaven has no barriers, our fears flew
Out death's window borne from life we grew
Onto smoky mountain heights where so few
Assemblages of innocent pass through.
Time's test: All that was old became new.

God:
Nice.

Day Ninety Six With God

Rabbi:

There are mountains between our love
Days multiplied into fruit market-dozens
I can measure distances how far you are
A star
A galaxy
A sunset with no horizon left to show
I found it exacerbating that when we married, you were
thousand miles from my mind.. I thought of a palm tree and
some monkeys squabbling on the branches.
I said "I do" to thin air between us and never meant a word of
faithfulness in my heart.
Now, years later I celebrate leaving you in divorce anniversaries
reaching over fifty.
If you can imagine being lost on the ocean in an inner tube, well
there you are passing right over me in your huge liner and I am
not trying in any way to signal you.
We spend all our days avoiding remembering shallow love.
And, when I ask myself, what did I see in you?
Well my answer is that I did not see you at all.
I was blind and still am when I think of you.

God:
You have issues.

Day Ninety Seven With God

Rabbi:
I have been in a rather sour mood lately.

God:
I have noticed.

Rabbi:
I am thinking about too many things and I cannot get to sleep.

God:
What is the reason?

Rabbi:
Age?

God:
Yea.

Rabbi:
Life is so comfortable. I have money, good health, days busy
with writing and doing tax returns.

God:
Pretty lucky.

Rabbi:
Something is missing. I do not like taking vacations.

Maybe this series on talking to you is troublesome. I almost
have one hundred poems and then I will stop and go on to
another project.

God:
I will miss you.

Rabbi:
You think that is my problem? Finishing these poems with you
as the respondent?

God:
No matter what you go on to do, I will be here to help you.

Rabbi:
Thank you so much.

Day Ninety Eight With God

Rabbi:

Over and Over

Diamond encloses bases chakras of what makes you tick
Deep inside that stomach you push into adversaries
A white light squishes out in protuberance
As skull point umpires start
I am interested in your heart
Because I am stuck on second
Two out three-two
Chakras divide us
An argument ensues
Fans do not like the last call
Game ends with a drainage
The sports writers fold up their portables
Bat boy picks up what has not been taken away
I look to tomorrow
When, maybe, I will get words
In edgewise
And start
Incarnation
Recurring
Over and
Over in translation

God:
Nice.

Day Ninety Nine With God

Rabbi:

Aqua Dreaming

she had never felt as naked
unable to move her hands
to cover herself, she closed her eyes
trying to free her mind from his hands
moving over her body like an invasion of her skin

she pretended that this was not happening
letting his touches become the wind on a beach
caressing her unwillingness as if she was a saint
enduring punishment for sins she never committed

moaning like a wild beast
she made sounds she never imagined
for her submission she thought of a god who would free her
letting a fantasy of forgetfulness
scene by scene progressing as a movie
she was a blind pilgrim caught unwillingly by a devil

along a tree draped shore line
she was a turtle returning to the sea
a frantic fish struggling to find water

God:
Nice.

Day One Hundred With God

Rabbi:
This poem brings an end to my days with God.

God:
I will miss you.

Rabbi:
I will miss you too.

Shakespeare had his chorus.
Plato had his voice.
Being with God is like Waiting For Godot.
I cover myself in prayer
I am naked in sin
I bless myself to draw God's blessing.
You have been my antiphon.
My psalms of simplicity.
Blessed be the poet for they shall play scrabble with words.

The Earth has an engine turning it accurately around the sun.
The sun has a place in our galaxy spinning around inside its orbit.
History has the poet bringing relief to the downtrodden.
Bringing hope to the faint-of-heart.

>This is my prayer:
>That cosmos and stars
>Find some peace when
>The universe contracts.

God:
Slow down.

Rabbi:
That earth will find a companion in the swirl of stars,
That souls will find peace within their anxieties.

God:
So long my friend.

Author's Biography

Michael Thomas is a CPA residing and working in Sterling Heights, Michigan who is best described as a warm and cuddly curmudgeon. He has been writing for decades, primarily poetry and short stories, but has a love of plays and theatre. Mostly, he defies description, not because he is nondescript, but because the proper words have not been invented. Those who know him well will tell you he is well worth knowing, and that is the best biography one can have.

Also by Michael Thomas

Rabbi Schlotz Stories

Michael Thomas

ISBN: 978-1500192037

The
Plantagenets

Henry II

Queen Eleanor

Michael Thomas

ISBN: 978-1492297567

Michael Thomas

The Accounting Book

ISBN: 978-1500267889

New Selected Writings

Writings

of

Michael Thomas

ISBN-13: 978-1530832071

ISBN: 978-1492776932

Michael Thomas Poetry
Volume 2

ISBN: 978-1495419010

Michael Thomas Poetry
Volume 3

ISBN-13: 978-1501063275

ISBN: 978-1507634387

Michael Thomas Poetry
Volume 5

ISBN: 978-1514174104

Michael Thomas Poetry
Volume 6

ISBN-13:978-1523266333

Michael Thomas Poetry
Volume 7

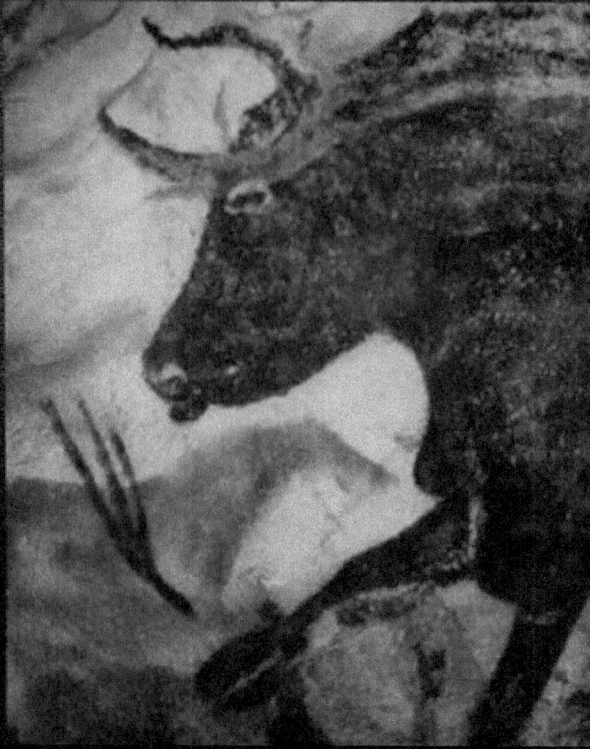

ISBN-13: 978-1-943974-13-9

Michael Thomas Poetry
Volume 8

ISBN: 978-1943974252

These and other books by independent authors
can be found at:

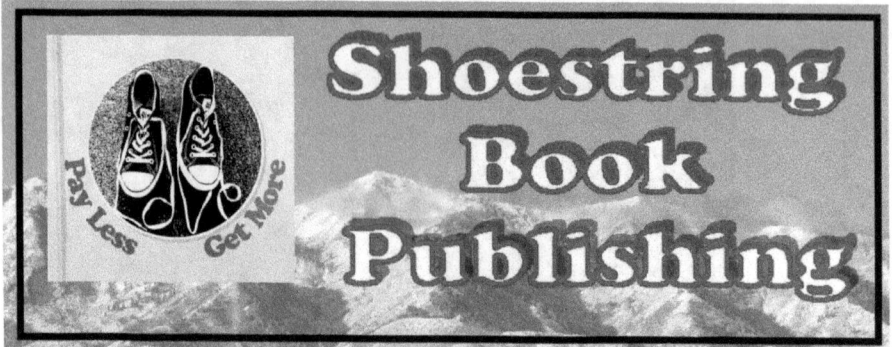

Please Review!

All independent authors depend upon reviews left on Amazon.com by readers to help promote their books. Without these reviews, they will hardly get any notice. Please take the time to leave a short review. Simply go to Amazon.com, find the book and go to the book's page. Under the author's name will be a list of reviews and stars. Click here and there will be a big button saying "Create your own review". Please click here and review.

It only takes a minute!

www.ingramcontent.com/pod-product-compliance
Lightning Source LLC
LaVergne TN
LVHW052020080426
835513LV00018B/2098